PENGUIN BOO⌐

BUT WAIT, TH⌐

Suzanne Paul grew up in the working-class poverty of England, determined to escape the miserable streets of Wolverhampton. She arrived
in New Zealand aged thirty-five with just eighteen dollars in her purse,
no job, no qualifications and no prospects. Against the odds, within five
years she became a successful businesswoman and a multimillionaire.
She went on to have her own hit TV shows, becoming a household
name, one of the country's much-loved celebrities and a motivational
speaker.

In 2005, due to several bad investments and a failed marriage, Suzanne
lost everything and was declared bankrupt. At fifty years of age Suzanne
had hit rock bottom, but instead of giving up, which she felt like doing
many times, she picked herself up and started again with nothing.

In 2007 Suzanne was crowned winner in the TV show *Dancing with
the Stars*, competing against women half her age. She is now happily
married and is busy rebuilding her empire, selling her own range of
cosmetics, shoes and clothes as well as a grocery range.

www.suzannepaul.co.nz

BUT WAIT, THERE'S MORE

Suzanne Paul

To Pam
Follow your dreams
and Fake it till you
make it !

Suzanne Paul

PENGUIN BOOKS

PENGUIN BOOKS

Published by the Penguin Group

Penguin Group (NZ), 67 Apollo Drive, Rosedale,
North Shore 0632, New Zealand (a division of Pearson New Zealand Ltd)
Penguin Group (USA) Inc., 375 Hudson Street,
New York, New York 10014, USA
Penguin Group (Canada), 90 Eglinton Avenue East, Suite 700, Toronto,
Ontario, M4P 2Y3, Canada (a division of Pearson Penguin Canada Inc.)
Penguin Books Ltd, 80 Strand, London, WC2R 0RL, England
Penguin Ireland, 25 St Stephen's Green,
Dublin 2, Ireland (a division of Penguin Books Ltd)
Penguin Group (Australia), 250 Camberwell Road, Camberwell,
Victoria 3124, Australia (a division of Pearson Australia Group Pty Ltd)
Penguin Books India Pvt Ltd, 11, Community Centre,
Panchsheel Park, New Delhi – 110 017, India
Penguin Books (South Africa) (Pty) Ltd, 24 Sturdee Avenue,
Rosebank, Johannesburg 2196, South Africa

Penguin Books Ltd, Registered Offices: 80 Strand, London, WC2R 0RL, England

First published by Penguin Group (NZ), 2008

1 3 5 7 9 10 8 6 4 2

Copyright © Suzanne Paul, 2008

The right of Suzanne Paul to be identified as the author of this work in terms of section
96 of the Copyright Act 1994 is hereby asserted.

Designed by Anna Egan-Reid
Typeset by Pindar NZ
Printed in Australia by McPherson's Printing Group

ISBN 978 014 301005 0

A catalogue record for this book is available
from the National Library of New Zealand.

www.penguin.co.nz

This book is dedicated to my
husband Duncan.

Your unconditional love and support
gives me strength every day
and makes anything seem possible.

Contents

This poem was sent to me a couple of years ago by a lovely old gent by the name of Arch McLachlan and I think it sums things up nicely.

Thanks, Arch

x

DON'T QUIT

When things go wrong, as they sometimes will,
When the road ahead seems all uphill.
When the funds are low and the debts are high,
and you want to smile, but you have to sigh.
When care is pressing you down a bit,
Rest if you must, but don't you quit.

Life is strange with its twists and turns,
As everyone of us sometimes learns.
And many a failure turns about,
When you might have won had you stuck it out.
Don't give up though the pace seems slow,
You may succeed with another blow.

Success is failure turned inside out,
The silver tint of the clouds of doubt.
And you can never tell how close you are,
It may be near, when it seems so far.

So stick to the fight when you are hardest hit,
It is when things seem worst that you must not quit!

author unknown

Introduction

When I arrived in New Zealand in 1991 I had eighteen dollars in my pocket and a dream of a better life. I was single and thirty-five years old, with no job, no qualifications and no prospects. I'd left all my family and friends behind in England in search of fame and fortune. I found both.

I became a partner and managing director of the country's most successful direct-marketing company and a household name, starring in my own TV shows. Within five years the company was sold for thirty-nine million dollars, I drove a

Mercedes convertible, lived in a six-million-dollar mansion and spent weekends on my luxury yacht with my toy-boy husband.

In March 2005, I was declared bankrupt and my whole world fell apart. At nearly fifty years of age, once again I had no home, no money and no future. I felt helpless and frightened and so low I was ashamed to hold my head up in public. I was afraid to answer the phone or open the mail – I hit rock bottom.

But instead of giving up, which I felt like doing many times, I picked myself up and started all over again with nothing.

Despite numerous setbacks I have managed to repay several creditors and get an early discharge out of bankruptcy. I've relaunched New Zealand's best-selling make-up, Natural Glow, and the Suzanne Paul shopping website.

I'm now building an empire encompassing clothes, shoes and accessories, as well as cosmetics and a range of groceries. Last year, against all odds, I danced to victory with a fractured rib and won *Dancing with the Stars*.

I've been to hell and back and twice round the roundabout, and I know how to go from rags to riches. I also know that if you can dream it, you can live it.

With this book you'll find out how to turn your dreams into reality, and have more fun in your life than you can shake a stick at. So start reading and start dreaming and I'll show you how to do the rest.

1

What do you want and why?

On my first day at Pendeford High School, I realised my family didn't have the sorts of things other families had. I realised I was different when a girl sat down next to me in the classroom and started moaning about her dad not letting her use the telephone after school. I sympathised and agreed it was unfair and told her my dad was the same.

But the truth was I had no idea how she felt. We didn't have a telephone and, up until then, I didn't know anyone else who did. Certainly no one down our street had one.

The area I grew up in was a typical working-class suburb of Wolverhampton in the West Midlands, called Whitmore Reans. Every house looked pretty much the same. Come to think of it, every street looked pretty much the same. There was row upon row of terraced houses, only interrupted by the occasional grocery store, pub or factory. Up until I was eleven I thought everyone lived that way.

Like all the other families down our street we didn't have a bath or a shower, and there was only a cold-water tap in the kitchen. Sunday nights we'd boil up kettles of hot water so we could have a rub down with a wet flannel in front of the fire, ready for school the next day. The only thing I hated was going down to the bottom of the yard to go to the toilet at night, especially when it was raining. Trying to balance an umbrella in one hand and a torch in the other while going to the loo was a nightmare. There were a couple of resident big black hairy spiders living in the corners, too, that I was always terrified of. I thought they were going to drop on me. Mind you, I'd have been in the right place if they had!

Even from an early age I loved performing. I'd put a variety of chairs and dustbins out in the backyard and charge all the kids in the street a penny a seat to watch me sing and dance wearing me mum's old clothes and shoes. I don't think there could have been much other entertainment in our neighbourhood – they all used to come!

I ended up at Pendeford High School because of my older brother Phillip, who was the brainy one in the family. He had passed his eleven-plus exams and he was given a place there. By the time it was my turn to take the same exam, it had been done away with. Because they liked to keep siblings together I got in there as well. The only problem was, it was quite a journey to get there and our family didn't have a car. Phillip and I had to go on two buses each way and when we got off the second bus going to school, the landscape had changed. We were in a different world — an upper-middle-class area, which felt to me like a different country.

I was able to bluff my way through the school days by pretending I lived the same way the other girls did. When they talked about their fancy clothes, I told them about mine. When they flashed their holiday snaps around at lunchtime, I said our camera had broken. When they asked for my telephone number I said Dad was strict and wouldn't let me use the phone — it was for business calls only.

That first year of high school I became quite an actress. Every day at school I discussed my imaginary life with my classmates. I never even told them I just lived with my dad and brother, as it was unheard of in those days to only have one parent. I talked about my mum as though she were still there doing the cooking and washing and ironing. In reality, she'd walked out on us years ago, when my father's domineering ways got too much for her.

Another reason I never mentioned Mum leaving was that I always thought she'd be coming back. She'd left once before when I was about eight, and was gone for several months. Then, one day, our neighbour from across the road called me into her house — me dad had asked her to wash my hair, because Mum was coming home. I remember being so excited I couldn't keep still, as Betty tried to comb the knots out of my thin and tatty hair.

For a few weeks, at least, everything in the garden seemed rosy. But it wasn't long before the arguing and shouting resumed. As a child I always thought the rows were because of my brother or me — because we'd been naughty. In those days, children were to be seen and not heard — there were no family discussions. We

> I would beg and plead with Dad to let me have some money — I hated being poor.

just did as we were told and tried to keep out of the way, in case we got in the firing line.

So, as I say, when I came home from school one day and found Mum had packed up her things and left again, I chose to believe me dad when he said she'd soon be back. For months after she'd gone I couldn't wait to get home, convinced she was going to be standing there in the kitchen cooking us something delicious for tea, but she never was. It was just a cold, dark, empty house. Because Dad used to work shifts at the factory, when we got home from school Phillip and I took it in turns to clean out the grate, build a coal fire and make something to eat.

When Dad was home he would sit and cry for hours and beg us not to leave as well — it was a sad, miserable existence for us all.

The only joy I found was at my local Church Hall where, from the age of eight, I went once a week for dancing lessons. For just a few pence I could escape into a magical world where I didn't have to worry about clean clothes for school, or how to patch the holes in my shoes — I just danced and laughed. I didn't have to pretend with the girls in the dancing class — we were from the same background. One day me dad marched in and announced that Mum had left and someone else would have to help me with my costumes.

Apart from the competitions, every year the dance school used to put a show on and we would be in several dances each. Sometimes the whole troupe would perform, plus there were duets and, if you were good enough, you might even get to do a solo performance. I wasn't good enough.

Occasionally one of the other mums would take pity on me and buy a bit of extra material and run me up a taffeta skirt while she was making one for her own daughter. Then I would sit at home sewing sequins on for hours, instead of doing my homework. Afterwards I would feel so embarrassed when, week after week, they kept asking me for the money for the material. I would beg and plead with Dad to let me have some money – I hated being poor.

When the mothers got fed up with all the drama of it, my friend Torchy started making costumes for me.

Her name wasn't really Torchy – it was Gill and she used to live up the street from me and, occasionally, she came to dancing classes. Our mums were friends and we grew up together. There was only a year between us. We were two snotty-nosed kids playing in the street together. When we were teenagers Gill dyed her hair blonde, except it went a peculiar shade of yellow. She looked like a cartoon character on TV at the time called 'Torchy' – hence the nickname, which stuck. We're both 50-year-old women now, but I still call her Torchy.

Torchy's mum had an old Singer sewing machine that you operated with your foot and Torchy tried to help me out by running up a few costumes for me. Sometimes it was better than nothing. We never seemed to get it quite right, which wasn't so bad if there were twenty of us on stage and we all looked slightly different, but if there were only half a dozen performers my badly made frocks looked pitiful.

On one occasion I was thrilled to be chosen to do a tap dance with two other girls and I practised for hours and hours. We all agreed it was our favourite dance and we couldn't wait to perform it. But Theresa, the dance teacher, took one look at me and said we couldn't go out on stage with me looking such a state. The other two girls had full swirly skirts covered in sequins. Mine was much shorter and quite straight – we didn't have enough material for anything else – with only about 20 sequins on it. I was also wearing my old school socks, held up with bits of elastic.

The other girls' mums wanted to know why we hadn't done our tap dance and everyone was really annoyed with me for not having the right outfit. I felt the shame burning into me. When I got home that night I cried so hard, I thought my heart would break. I did get to do a solo performance before I left dancing school for good. We put on a Christmas show at the Grand Theatre in Wolverhampton and I did a character song and dance from the musical *Fiddler on the Roof*. I think the dance teacher chose that for me because I didn't have to wear a fancy costume – just me brother's old clothes. But it was the best feeling in the world standing on that stage belting out 'If I Were a Rich Man' with Mum sitting in the audience. I wasn't the best singer in the show, but I sang my heart out just the same.

The dancing lessons were also a great excuse to use at school that first year, to get out of doing something or going somewhere. The other girls would invite me to go up the local shopping centre on a Saturday night, or to meet them at the movies or a coffee shop, but I would conjure up a dance competition or exam or some fictitious show I was performing in that very same day.

I desperately wanted to be in the 'in crowd' but I knew I'd end up the laughing stock if I went out in my unfashionable old clothes to someone's party. At least inside those school gates I looked as though I fitted in – we all had the same uniform on.

Mind you, at the start of the following year it became perfectly obvious to everyone that our family didn't have the ready cash that they all did. Phillip and I turned up the first day of the new term to discover everyone in new school uniforms. I was wearing the same uniform when I left school four years later as the day I started. It was our Phil I used to really feel sorry for. He had shot up really quickly and the sleeves of his jacket were halfway up his arms – he used to look a right idiot.

Mind you, I was no oil painting with my milk-bottle thick, National Health glasses perched crookedly on my nose. They were forever lopsided as they were held together with either sticky tape or sticking plaster. It was not a great look on a painfully thin, scruffy twelve year old. I recently asked Phillip how he remembers me looking back then, and he said, 'Knobbly. Everything about you was knobbly – from your knobbly nose to your knobbly knees.' Charming!

Needless to say, I never liked school, I always felt different – like a second-class citizen. The teachers didn't help matters either. I remember one time I was so excited about going on a school trip to the Yorkshire Potteries and when we got there the teacher made me stay on the coach as I hadn't paid any money for the trip. I wanted the floor to swallow me up as the other kids all pushed past me to get off and I promised myself that, one day, I'd have more money than the rest of them put together, and I did.

I just about managed to keep the bullies from tormenting me by playing the class clown. I'd discovered at quite an early age that I could make people laugh. I'd inherited my father's caustic wit, which came in handy on many occasions. One time I was walking home from the bus stop when a gang of local girls blocked my path and I knew I was in for a good hiding. I looked at the meanest one and said, 'What's up with your mate? She's got a face a dog wouldn't lick.' Luckily, that did it. She cracked up laughing and they let me go home.

By the time I was thirteen I'd had enough of school. While the other girls seemed to get prettier every year, I just got even more gawky-looking and I couldn't wait to leave. By the time I was fifteen, I was playing truant every week and the school sent several letters to me dad saying if it carried on I would be expelled. He never saw the letters, because I always made sure I got to the mail first, just in case. But I knew he'd go off his trolley if I got expelled, so I went to see the careers officer to find out what my job options were. She said, 'Shop assistant or factory worker', but I didn't really fancy either.

I had no idea what I wanted to be and no idea what I could be. I just knew I wanted to get the hell out of Wolverhampton and be rich and famous. Just the getting out of Wolverhampton turned out to be the hardest part.

What do you want and why?

I'm surprised at the number of people I talk to who don't know what they want.

If you don't know what you want, how are you going to get it?

If you don't know where you want to go, how are you going to get there?

I was no smarter than any other girl in our town. I was certainly no luckier or prettier. The only difference was, I knew what I wanted and they didn't. Or, maybe, by the time they figured out what they wanted they thought it was too late.

That's rubbish! There's no age limit on getting what you want. The only thing stopping you from leading the life you want to, is you.

Motivation

To make your dreams a reality you have stay motivated, otherwise you'll give up when the going gets tough. When you figure out exactly what you want you'll have the determination to succeed. Knowing the reasons WHY you want something will give you the motivation to achieve it.

You don't have to know how you're going to achieve things. When you work out what you want and why, your brain will work out how later.

When you have a strong enough reason for doing something, you can figure out how to do it. You have a motive. For example, if your goal is to lose weight, then you need to think of all the reasons why you want to, such as:

- You'll have more confidence.
- You can buy all new clothes.
- You'll look fabulous on holiday in a bikini.
- You'll be healthier and full of energy.
- Your kids won't be ashamed of you.

If you remember these reasons whenever you're tempted to pig out, you'll have enough motivation to eat less and move more. You will lose all the weight you want and reach your goal!

Blackmail

Some people need an incentive as their motivation to keep going. For example, if you want to keep your teenagers studying hard so they pass their exams, a reward is a great incentive. It might be a car, driving lessons or a holiday. Whatever it is, make sure you keep talking about it in great detail so that they keep motivated.

Many companies use a bonus as an incentive to get employees to work harder or to do more overtime, but when you're looking for a big enough reason to pursue your own goals don't use money as your motive. Instead think about what having the money will do for you:

- You could travel and see the world.
- You could look after family and friends.
- You could buy a house in the country and have peace and quiet.
- You would never have to worry about paying the bills ever again.

I didn't want to settle
for a good life,
I was aiming for a
great life!

On days when you feel like you can't go on, bring all of your motives into mind and they will fill you with enough energy and enthusiasm to give it another go!

The memory of those hard, lonely years growing up in Wolverhampton gave me all the motivation I needed to keep going, when all I wanted to do was give up. I kept going, not because I wanted the same as the other girls, but because I wanted more. I wanted better clothes, a bigger house, a more expensive car. I wanted more money than they'd ever see in their lives. More than anything I wanted to show them all I wasn't a second-class citizen and I wasn't going to be that girl left sitting on the coach while everyone else had fun.

I didn't want to settle for a good life, I was aiming for a great life!

Even now, thirty-five years later, the idea of going back to Wolverhampton and living that way again is enough to make me try to move mountains.

Notes

2

If you can dream it, you can live it!

So I left school at the age of fifteen with no qualifications and got a job as an office junior. It was mainly filing, collecting the post and sending out invoices, for which I was paid three pounds a week. It was a measly sum even in those days. I soon got bored and decided to give shop work a go – it was much better paid and you weren't looking at the same old faces day after day.

It's funny how circumstances can affect different people in different ways. As soon as he could, my brother Phillip set about creating the perfect family life to make up for the lousy one he'd had growing up. He was brainy enough to go to university but, instead, he got a good job in the laboratory at the Royal Hospital in town and studied part time. Like me he was tired of being scruffy and broke and wanted to earn his own money straight away, but unlike me he wanted to settle down and have a family. I couldn't think of anything worse.

Watching the disintegration of my parents' marriage had completely put me off the idea of walking down the aisle in a white frock, even though I was surrounded by girls who thought the only way to improve their circumstances was by marrying 'above their station'.

I didn't even know how you were supposed to meet these rich men – there certainly weren't any up at the local disco.

I remember going to a dance one night with Torchy and a few others. We'd decided to go somewhere different, to try and meet a better class of person. There was a live band playing at the Civic Hall. The only way I could get into town was on the bus and I knew by the time I got there my long wavy hair would be hanging like rats' tails. So I put my rollers in, put a scarf over the top, and got on the bus like that, in my long red evening dress. When I arrived I dashed straight to the loo to take the curlers out before anyone could see me.

I had a couple of dances with a fairly attractive man in a business suit and we were all convinced he must be a lawyer or a doctor or something equally posh. The other girls were getting very excited as he kept looking at me all night. He even bought me a drink – he must be rich! My heart was in my mouth as I saw him striding over at the end of the night. I was sure I was about to get a lift home in a nice comfy car. My heart dropped down to my feet when he asked, 'Would you like to come back to my caravan? I've got pig's trotters on the boil!' I politely declined to the sound of Torchy's hysterical laughter. Needless to say, I never went to that dance hall again.

Here in New Zealand, things are much more integrated. You can have a five-million-dollar home plonked right next door to a state house. Every day poor people mix with rich people and if you had the right clothes on, nobody would be able to tell one from the other. But in 1960s Wolverhampton, you didn't mix outside of your social circle – it was simply unheard of.

Because of my neighbourhood and circumstances, I was raised to believe that doctors and lawyers were a level above me. I looked up to those people and it was a given that they would look down on me. I wasn't their equal and never would be.

Part of the problem was the variety of different accents to be found all over England. As soon as you opened your mouth everyone knew where you were from and what type of education and upbringing you'd had. My accent would have told the whole country that I was a common, working-class nobody. That's why I wanted to leave.

I thought my best chance of getting out of Wolverhampton and making something of myself, was by taking typing classes and becoming a secretary in a nice office in London. But everyone around me thought I'd completely lost my marbles. I soon found out, that when you're born into that working-class environment it's very difficult to get out.

Whenever I mentioned my desire to leave I'd be quickly reminded of who I was and where I came from. The reaction I got from people in my neighbourhood was negative and discouraging, to say the least. 'Who do you think you are? You've got a bob on your self,' they'd say. When I raised the idea of working and living somewhere else people would ask, 'Do you think you're better than us?' But how can you say to people 'I don't want to be like you'? It was as if no one wanted me to have a better life.

You weren't expected to have any grand ambitions of getting rich, travelling the world or living anywhere but in the town you were born in. No one had dreams or goals. They just went to work, paid the bills and put their names down on the waiting list for a council house.

So, I gave up on the idea of becoming a secretary and became a sales assistant in a menswear shop instead, and I loved it! It was the early 1970s and bell-bottomed trousers, bright-patterned shirts and wide lapels were all the rage. Denim was big and so was corduroy and I thought I was the bee's knees standing there every day with my new trendy glasses on. Our Phil had bought them for me out of one of his first wage packets – bless him. I'd managed to buy myself a couple of nice outfits, too, so life was looking good. I even had me a boyfriend.

People say you never forget your first love, and they're right. He swept me off my feet and then ripped my heart out. I was sweet sixteen and at twenty-three he seemed worldly and sophisticated – he even had a car. We met one Sunday night when, as usual, I was sitting in the launderette just up the road from our house, doing the weekly wash. He'd moved into the flat opposite and we got chatting while we watched the threadbare towels go round and round. To say I worshipped the ground he walked on would be putting it mildly. I think he found me amusing, but the relationship was destined to fail. A year later he put a note through the letterbox telling me it was all over and he didn't want to see me anymore – what a piece of work he was.

But life went on and at least in my job I'd found something that I was good at – selling. Over the next few years I moved from shop to shop selling everything from clothes and shoes to camping equipment and confectionary. I loved the challenge of selling. I didn't mind what the product was. Mostly, I loved the

> *I loved every minute of my Butlins experience. It was easy and stress free — it felt like being on holiday all the time.*

people contact, but I found that once I'd been in a shop for three or four months I would get bored and want to move on. It was still my dream to escape the dreary streets of Wolverhampton.

I was eighteen when I came up with the idea of working at a Butlins holiday camp. Butlins have a chain of camps in seaside towns all over England, and I applied to be a shop assistant at the one in Filey, Yorkshire. I was so excited when I found out I'd got the job, but I was also terrified. For the first time, I was going on my own and didn't know what to expect. The job entitled me to three meals a day plus free chalet accommodation — it sounded like heaven to me.

When I first saw the chalet I was to be living in for the next six months, I sat down on the bed and cried. It was as much out of fear and loneliness as anything else. It looked more like a broom cupboard it was so small — just two single beds separated by a sink. The bath and toilet were housed in a separate block at the other end of the staff quarters. It was even further to walk to the loo than at home!

I was just thinking that I wouldn't bother unpacking my case as it appeared I'd gone from bad to worse, when the door flew open and in walked my chalet mate. She told me her name was Deidre and that she'd left a good job as a piccalilli stirrer to come and work at Butlins. I liked her immediately and decided to give it a go after all.

The next morning I leapt out of bed wondering what the hell was going on. A voice was booming from the loudspeaker up in the corner, 'Morning campers, time to get up. Today we've got the knobbly knees contest around the pool and the glamorous granny competition in the Princess Ballroom and I'd like to say a very happy birthday to Madge Smith.' It was certainly more effective and more annoying than an alarm clock.

I worked in the gift shop. It was quite big and similar to a department store, selling everything from sticks of rock to buckets and spades – the British love nothing more than sitting on the beach building sandcastles.

There were lots of counters but the shop was overstaffed, so the boss told me to grab a duster and tidy things up, but after half an hour of that I was so bored I thought I'd look for something else to do. I noticed that a man on the leather goods counter was really busy so I went up and asked if he needed any help. He introduced himself as Max and soon had me selling all sorts of leather knick-knacks, key rings and purses to the happy holidaymakers.

The next morning he came to find me and asked if I wanted to work on his counter again, permanently. Apparently, some of the stands were owned privately and employed their own staff. It meant I didn't have to wear the purple overall the other girls did and I would get paid more, plus there would be a bonus at the end of the summer season.

I loved every minute of my Butlins experience. It was easy and stress free – it felt like being on holiday all the time. We didn't have to worry about paying bills or cooking meals. We just went to work and the rest of the time we could enjoy the facilities of the camp. It was a wonderful carefree life and I had new friends from different towns and cities all over the country. The only problem was that at the end of the summer season the holiday camps closed and, all of a sudden, we were out of work and homeless.

I developed a routine of working in a Butlins camp over the

summer and going back to Wolverhampton for the winter. Instead of living with my dad again, I'd re-established contact with my mum and went to stay with her, my stepfather Bill and their young son, my brother Billy.

In my third season at Butlins, I was running all three of Max's counters at a camp in Minehead, Somerset. As well as leather goods, I was in charge of an engraving stand and a comb counter. Max had taught me how to engrave jewellery and print names on combs. People would come up and ask 'Have you got a blue comb with John on it?' or 'What about a red Peter?'. One memorable day, an elderly lady charged up to me and demanded to know if I had a pink Fanny! I was so taken aback I just stood there with my mouth hanging open, thinking I must have heard wrong. She said it again. I could feel a fit of the giggles coming on, so I ducked underneath the counter on the pretence of looking for one. So now I'm sitting on the floor with tears rolling down my face, convulsing with laughter while she's still shouting over the top, 'Have you got a pink Fanny or not?' Happy days!

Sometimes, in between seasons, instead of going back to Wolverhampton I'd go and find work and accommodation in another town. One year I fell for a lad from Batley, Yorkshire, and we spent the winter there, working in a wool mill. It was vile. There were rows upon rows of us all doing exactly the same thing, day in, day out, and the job was horrible. I had a big piece of wire mesh in front of me and on it would be a pile of felt material in little tiny bits. I had to sort it into groups of colour. It was a nightmare. After half an hour my glasses would be covered in fluff and it all looked the same to me in the dim lighting. I was always getting into trouble for putting the black bits in with the navy and the green bits in with the brown. But the worst thing about it was the mice. The fluff from the fabric fell through the mesh, into the tray underneath and the mice used to make their nests in it. Every morning before I could start sorting, I had to bang on the top with a stick, to make the mice run away. The noise of them scattering every which way used to make me feel sick. I couldn't wait to leave and get back to Butlins.

The only good thing to come out of living in Yorkshire was my life long obsession with Gene Pitney. I went to see him perform one night at Batley Variety Club and thought he had the most wonderful voice I'd ever heard. It reminded me of my dad, who had a beautiful singing voice – he used to perform regularly at the workingmen's clubs and would belt out a few songs at home when he'd had a couple of beers.

After that first night I went to see Gene perform dozens of times, in different towns all over England, and even got to meet him backstage on occasions and have a chat. My fondest memory is when he came to New Zealand and Mum and I had our photo taken with him. It's a treasured possession and we were both devastated when he died.

Occasionally, in between Butlins seasons, I'd have trouble finding shop work. Rather than signing on for the dole, I'd try my hand at something else. For a while I was a cinema usherette, in the days when they came round at half time selling choc-ices and fags. I think that would be a good idea again with movies being so long – but not the fags, of course. I was a meat-packer for a Tescos supermarket. I didn't enjoy that at all but the money was good so I did it for a while. And I was a sausage-linker for a day and a petrol-pump attendant for a couple of months.

I really would give anything a go.

If you can dream it, you can live it

I read that saying somewhere when I was a teenager. At the time I didn't know if it was true or not, but I've been testing the theory for the past thirty-odd years and you know what? It is true!

As I was growing up I dreamed of a better life. Every day I would sit for hours thinking about all the lovely things I was going to have – the clothes I would buy, the holidays I would take. I did it so often that, in seconds, I could conjure up a wonderful image of my life playing out in my mind in full glorious technicolour.

Everything I dreamed of having, I got. Then I lost it all again because I stopped dreaming. I stopped wanting.

I thought success was a destination and I was there. I found out that in fact, success was only part of the journey.

Dream big

Remember you can have whatever you want, so aim high.

DREAMS BECOME GOALS

GOALS BECOME PLANS

PLANS BECOME REALITY

Just sit and think about how you want your life to be.

How would you like your life to change over the next year?

You can live the life you want.

You have the power to turn anything you dream about into reality.

Whatever you
focus on,
you move toward.

Make a wish list

It's your life – be in control of it.

- What do you want to make happen?
- Where you want to live?
- Do you want to go back to studying?
- Would you love to play the piano or, maybe, learn another language?

Just sit and think about how you want your life to be. Then picture yourself living that life. In your mind, see yourself in your fabulous new home. Go for a walk around the beautiful garden and feel the sun on your face. Dive into your sparkling blue swimming pool, and feel the cool water invigorating you. As you feel the joy of it all, you are turning fantasy into fact because whatever you focus on, you move toward.

THE LAW OF ATTRACTION
The universe will make it happen.
You will be guided to meet the right people.
You will be in the right place at the right time.
You'll have marvellous ideas that will enable you to be
hugely successful in your chosen field.

Sounds airy fairy, doesn't it? I know, that's what I thought too, but it does work.

That doesn't mean you can just sit at home dreaming about your new car, waiting for someone to knock on the door and present you with one. It doesn't work like that. You have to put yourself out there, knowing that everything you desire is on its way.

But sometimes, while it's all happening behind the scenes, you're going to find yourself doing an unpleasant or boring job to pay the bills. I've had some crackers in my time, but whatever I've found myself doing to make a living, I've done the job the best I can with a smile on my face.

Someone always notices.

You're not going to meet anyone to help you reach your goals while you're sitting at home twiddling your thumbs. Instead of waiting for the perfect job to come along, have a go at something else, no matter how dull it may seem.

The worst that can happen is that you'll learn some new skills and come away with a great reference, plus it proves to future employers that you're a good, hard worker.

There are no coincidences – just the universe steering you in the right direction.

While you're out there earning a living, make sure you tell as many people as you can about your dreams and aspirations. I've lost count of the times somebody's said to me, 'What a coincidence, I know someone with an empty house you can stay at', or 'What a coincidence, my father's looking for someone to work in his new store, and it's right on the beach'.

All you have to do is something. Whatever it is, do it to the very best of your abilities and then some!

Notes

3

Fake it till you make it

One year, I decided to give Israel a go and my family nearly had me committed! At the end of the summer season I saw an ad in the paper, looking for people to go and work in Israel. I'd never been abroad before, so I called the number and arranged to go to London to meet the company organising the whole thing. I had to pay the airfare and a small fee, and they would arrange for someone to pick me up when I arrived and take me to the kibbutz where I was to live and work for six months. I couldn't wait.

Two weeks later I was on a plane to Israel with a bunch of like-minded souls who'd also signed up for the adventure. On first inspection the kibbutz I was assigned to seemed similar to Butlins, but hotter. I shared a room with two other women and the shower block was along the way. All meals were provided in the dining room. Young people came from all over the world to experience the kibbutz way of life. The permanent residents – the kibbutzniks – all received the same wage no matter what job they did. When the kibbutz made a profit from the orange crop it was shared equally among them all.

The other aspect I found unusual was how the children lived apart from their parents in specially designed houses. I was sent to work in one of the baby houses helping to care for four gorgeous little two year olds. I thought it was the best job going. There was always another caregiver present because I didn't speak the language, but after a few months working there I could speak fluent Hebrew – well, as fluent as a two-year-old, anyway. The children were all from different families and the parents would come to visit them twice a day, and have them to stay of a weekend. I loved the job, but after three months they moved me to work in the orange groves, which I thought sounded very exciting but turned out to be really hard work. Because of the heat we had to start early in a morning, usually arriving in the fields about 6 am when everything was still wet with dew. Some of the oranges grew on very low bushes, which meant you had to crawl into the middle of a bush to get at the oranges. The spiders there were huge and I used to be scared to death, as all manner of creepy crawlies fell on my head or went down my top. You could see women up and down the line jumping about, ripping their clothes off and shrieking, trying to dislodge something disgusting. I used to dread going to work. So I put my name down to operate one of the machines they used to pick oranges from the top of the tall trees. They were a bit like the contraptions you see men fixing the traffic lights with, you pressed a button and the box you were standing in would raise up,

> *I could speak fluent Hebrew — well, fluent as a two-year-old, anyway.*

go left or right, and you could drive forwards or backwards. It was a sought-after job, though a bit dangerous. I was lucky that a machine shortly became vacant. Not so lucky the girl who vacated it – she had broken her leg in the process!

Because the machines had two wheels at the back and only one at the front, you could easily tip over if one wheel went in a ditch. I only had one accident on mine, and I was thrown through the air. Luckily, I landed in a tree and not on the ground. But I was hanging up there for a good thirty minutes before someone came to rescue me. Still, it was better than crawling about with spiders.

The kibbutz was a wonderful experience and I went back again a couple of years later and stayed for a whole year. On my return I was sad to hear that one of the boys I had looked after had died in a car crash, and I went to visit his mother. We looked at pictures of us all laughing in the sunshine. I cried because little Ran was dead, and I cried because she was in a wheelchair and I cried because she'd been driving the car. It's funny how life can turn on a sixpence.

One dreary winter, I found myself back in Wolverhampton living with Mum, Bill and little Billy, who was then about eight years old. They were running a greengrocers shop and we all lived above it, in a large three-bedroom flat. Even though it was very noisy of a night – there was also a fish and chip shop underneath us – I really enjoyed living there. We had a washing machine, a telephone and, best of all, an inside toilet. I thought I'd really gone up in the world!

I don't know the ins and outs of it, but the next minute we were all living in a poky caravan, in the middle of a field stuck out in the country! One minute you're going great guns then you look around and it's all turned to custard. I felt like I was drowning in a big pot of it. Now we didn't even have a toilet, just a chemical bucket in a shed outside. I used to heave whenever I got anywhere near it. My stomach turns even now, just thinking about it. We couldn't get a council house – there was a waiting list for them. So we had to stay in the caravan until we found something we could afford to rent.

At the time, I was working in a department store in the centre of town selling and engraving ballpoint pens. We were really busy with it being the Christmas period. I loved the job and it was quite well paid – I was receiving a basic wage plus commission on the number of pens sold.

However, being stuck in the country meant I had to set off each morning, while it was still dark, to be at the store for opening time. The only way to reach the village to catch the bus into town was to walk along a dirt track, beside the canal. My heart would be pounding as I inched my way along in my big black wellies. It would either be raining or snowing and the pathway was dangerously slippery and sludgy.

I don't know what terrified me more – the thought of falling into the murky, grey water, or that some man would grab hold of me and I'd never be seen again. After an hour on the bus, I'd arrive at work looking like a bedraggled rag-bag, and feeling worn out before the day had even started. I think the worst thing was knowing I'd have to do it all again at the end of the day – there was not much to look forward to.

It always seems to me, that when I hit rock bottom and life

seems too hard, that is the exact point when everything changes again. It's like the universe is saying, 'Well, you made a right mess there. Let's send a few opportunities your way – and a bit of good luck, too.'

This time, my good luck was called Joy. One miserable day she set up her counter next to mine and the sun came out. Joy was demonstrating a metal polish called Mista Bright. She attracted a huge crowd that seemed to hang on her every word as though they were hypnotised. She would throw the jar of polish in the air, talk about what it could do and show how it worked. At the same time, she would be laughing and joking with people, and I'd never seen anything like it. It was like watching live theatre and I found it absolutely fascinating.

One day, while Joy was on a tea break a customer came and asked me if I could show her how the polish worked. I said I didn't really know much about it, but I'd have a go. I stood behind her counter and found myself saying, 'It cleans silver, silverplate, brass, copper, bronze, pewter, chrome, stainless steel and aluminium. But wait, there's more.' I did the whole spiel from start to finish and sold her a jar of Mista Bright at the end!

I hadn't realised that I'd learned the demonstration word for word, parrot fashion, while Joy had been saying it over and over for the last few months, day in and day out. When I turned round there she was with a big smile on her face, saying, 'You're very good. If you want, I can get you a job at the Ideal Home Exhibition in London. It's working for a lovely couple and it's really good money.' I didn't need to be asked twice!

The pen engraving had only been a temporary stand over Christmas. I was going to be out of work in the New Year anyway, so it was perfect timing. The Ideal Home Show ran for the whole month of March and it turned out to be a major turning point in my life. The company that sold Mista Bright was owned by an elderly couple called Anna and George, who also had an antique shop in Brighton. They were lovely people who took me under their wing and showed me great kindness.

That first day, when I walked into the exhibition hall I was gobsmacked. The Earls Court Centre was enormous, there were stands as far as the eye could see. I was completely blown away. There were even several show homes there, too. You could have gone round the Home Show every day for a week and still not have seen everything. It was an incredible sight. I would be working every day, from ten in the morning until ten at night, for four weeks. I was so excited, I was beside myself.

The stand was in a prime position and there were eight Mista Bright girls standing behind a long counter, each demonstrating how the polish worked. The stand always attracted a lot of attention because of the beautiful crystal and silverware displays brought from Anna and George's antique shop.

That first week I thought it was a doddle – all you had to do was keep saying the same thing over and over again and smiling and laughing. It was hardly rocket science. The second week I was starting to sound like a worn-out record and by the third week I was bored out of my brains. So were all the punters, standing in front of me. As we were only paid commission on the polish we sold, I wasn't earning as much as the other girls and I wasn't very happy about it.

I went to see Anna. 'I don't think I'm cut out for this lark. It's easy for Joy and the other girls – they're having a great time and selling loads,' I said. 'I don't have the energy to carry on and I certainly don't feel like laughing and joking.'

Anna told me something then that I've never forgotten, something that's seen me through some terrible times and still does. She said, 'Those girls don't want to be here any more than you do. They're also feeling tired and fed up but the difference is, they're pretending they're having a great time and you're not. Every time you say that demonstration, it has to sound like it's the first time you've ever said it. You have to laugh when people make the same old joke. You have to keep smiling and pretending you're having a ball.

'When you feel like you can't go on, just close your eyes, take a deep breath, then open your eyes wide and smile and just get on with it!' That afternoon, I spent twenty minutes doing a demo and the whole crowd walked off without buying anything. But instead of standing there with a face like thunder feeling pissed off, I decided I'd give Anna's method a go. I put on my 'performance face' and pretended I was full of energy and enthusiasm. I joked and laughed, and a funny thing happened while I was pretending to be so happy – I realised I wasn't pretending anymore. Somewhere along the way, my brain couldn't distinguish between what was real and what was imagined. I pretended I was having a great time, so I was.

Everything I know about the art of selling was taught to me by Anna and George that month at the Ideal Home Show: how to build a crowd and hold them; how to up-sell so the customer buys more; and how to talk from the diaphragm so that I didn't lose my voice. I also learned that you never give up, no matter how many people say no. That just means you are one step closer to someone saying yes.

Joy was right – the money was good. At the end of the month I left with three thousand pounds in my pocket and I'd agreed to work several more exhibitions around the country selling Mista Bright. I was on top of the world.

Earning such excellent money had lulled me into a false sense of security. The next exhibition I worked at was in Birmingham. I thought it would be much the same as at Earls Court and expected to come away with another three thousand.

Unfortunately, hardly anybody came and I made very little money but, like a gambler, I was addicted. I thought the next exhibition would be the big one where I'd earn my fortune. The thought of earning the same kind of money as I had at Earls Court kept me going and you never knew which show would turn out to be a winner, so you had to do them all, just in case.

I spent the next ten years travelling around the United Kingdom working in various towns and cities, selling all sorts of products, for all sorts of companies. Besides Mista Bright, I peddled a vibrating massage pillow, a cream-maker, a portable steam iron, a magnetic window washer and a barking toy dog. I demonstrated stuff to clean your oven, your jewellery and your car. And I sold a variety of contraptions that would chip, chop, slice and dice every type of fruit or vegetable you can imagine. As well, there were things that would make you look thinner, younger, smarter and prettier than anyone else on the planet.

For all those years on the road, I was working for commission only. I never received a basic wage, sick pay or holiday pay and I was never paid travelling or accommodation expenses – if I didn't sell anything I didn't get any money.

I was like a gypsy, always on the move. If I wasn't working at an exhibition I was demonstrating in a department store for three or four months at a time. By then everyone in town would have seen the product and it would be time to move again.

> When I was up there on my stand, it was like being on the stage.

It was quite a lonely life – I was never in one place long enough to make any real friends. Still I was used to being lonely, and I thought it a small price to pay to reach my goals.

LEFT: Me and my big brother Phillip in the street where we grew up. I'm about seven.

BELOW: The Queen of the May Festival in Wolverhampton. I'm the one holding the train in the front.

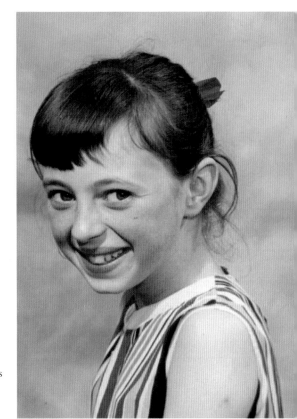

RIGHT: This is a school photo – I am about nine years old in this one.

BELOW: I'm eleven and it's my dancing class performance. I'm the one with short hair and knobbly knees standing at the end of the row on the left.

LEFT: Me and my little brother Billy in 1975.

BELOW: Me winning the Holiday Princess competition in 1981.

ABOVE: Me at Butlins Holiday Camp where I worked in the shop. I'm eighteen.

BELOW LEFT: Me selling prawns at Butlins.

BELOW RIGHT: Picking oranges in Israel.

ABOVE: Me and my friends celebrating the Silver Jubilee.

LEFT: My bunny girl days at Pontins Holiday Camp.

ABOVE: This photo appeared in the *Wolverhampton Express & Star*. I thought I'd hit the big time by having my photo in the local paper.

BELOW: Here I'm demonstrating diamond weight star point jewellery.

LEFT: Me as a hostess in the British pavilion at the Expo '88 in Brisbane.

BELOW: Me demonstrating at the Auckland Home Show.

ABOVE: Me and Paul Meier at the first pharmacy fair we ever did with Natural Glow.

RIGHT: Me and the girls out on the town.

I loved being a sales demonstrator. When I was up there on my stand, it was like being on the stage. I would put my 'performance face' on and entertain the crowd – it was even better if I managed to sell them something. I liked the excitement of turning up in a new town, selling a new product. I always thought, 'This is it. This is going to be great – I can feel it in me water!'

Sometimes things were marvellous and I earned a fortune, but other times I barely made enough to pay the rent and wondered how I'd survive. Part of the problem was being at the mercy of the department store managers. I wouldn't know where they were going to let me set up my stand, until I got there. If I was lucky, I'd get a fantastic position on the ground floor near the cosmetics and perfume. I was always going to do well in that location. Other times, when they were short of space, I'd be shoved down in the basement, behind the mops and buckets where you could fire a gun up the aisle and not hit anybody.

In between jobs I'd pop back to Wolverhampton to visit the family. My dad had moved into a small council flat while Mum and the two Bills were renting a house in the suburb of Walsall. Even though I didn't get on with my stepfather, me, Mum and young Billy managed to have a few laughs. I always enjoyed being home for Christmas when we would have a bit of a do. The only thing I didn't enjoy was having to listen to everyone my age going on about putting their names down for a council house or getting married and settling down. They thought I was quite mad with the dreams and schemes I had to make me rich.

One Christmas, I thought I was onto a real winner when I scored a job in a department store in Blackpool. It was one of my favourite places to live – there's nowhere quite like it anywhere in the world. From the kiss-me-quick hats to the donkey rides along the beach, it still has a certain tacky charm. Even though it was freezing there in the winter, with the icy wind blowing in across the North Sea, there are always plenty of tourists in town to see the Blackpool Illuminations. They've been a major attraction since 1879 and people travel from all over England to drive along the promenade with its twinkling, sparkling lights. It's called the Golden Mile, but it's more like seven miles long.

I was thrilled when I got a job as a candle dipper and demonstrator. It was the best fun I'd had in a long while, dipping the candles into layer upon layer of hot coloured wax, and the smell was delicious. I would then pass them onto the candle carver, who would carve wonderful patterns and shapes into them, revealing all the different layers underneath. Not surprisingly, they sold like hot cakes – hot candles.

I was looking forward to earning lots of money as it was getting busier every week – candles and Christmas are a perfect match. But once again, the rug was ripped out from under me. The store manager told us we had to move out because they were too busy and needed the space, but I think it was a bit more personal than that. He'd asked me out a few days before and I'd declined the offer. Was he that petty? Whatever the reason, I was out of work and couldn't find another job for love nor money.

I was living in a dingy bedsit – one room with a bed that also served as a couch, plus a cooker, a sink, an electric fire and a telly. I had a hamster called Miffy when I moved in, but he'd died. At least, I thought he'd died. Later, someone told me that hamsters hibernate when they're cold – I might have buried him alive!

It was certainly cold that year. It was the coldest winter on record and there was knee-deep snow everywhere. I don't think they've had snow in Blackpool before or since.

I'd paid the rent but didn't have enough money left for luxuries, such as electricity or food. I'd arranged to go to a friend's house for Christmas dinner, but we were snowed in and I couldn't get across town.

Instead, I lit all the candles left over from my dipping days, opened a tin of processed peas and huddled under my duvet to keep warm while I ate them.

The best thing about hitting rock bottom and realising that things really can't get any worse is that there's only one way to go from there and that's up. At that time, I was excited about the thought of having fifty pence to put in the electricity meter. I imagined all the lovely foods I'd eat and the programmes I'd watch on the telly once I started earning again. I had so much to look forward to – anything was going to be an improvement.

Even though I had to bend the truth a bit – actually I told a huge lie – to get my next job, the improvement was better than I could have hoped for. I felt I had no choice but to lie – desperate times called for desperate measures!

FAKE IT TILL YOU MAKE IT

Sometimes,
you need to fake it
until you make it.

Just do it!

At least, that's what the people at Nike say. The British have a different saying: Just get on with it!

Whatever way you say it, sometimes you just have to put a brave face on and do what needs to be done. Anna called it the 'performance face' and said I had to get out there and pretend. I've found it works every time.

YOUR BRAIN CAN'T TELL THE DIFFERENCE BETWEEN WHAT'S REAL AND WHAT'S IMAGINED

That's why, if you start thinking about something that annoyed the hell out of you last week, you get angry all over again. You feel the same emotions as when the incident first happened, as you go over it all in your mind. Your brain can't distinguish between what's real and what's not and thinks it's all happening again.

How you think affects how you feel.

How you feel affects how you act.

So, if you act differently you get different results.

That sounds like common sense really, when you think about it. The problem is, when we're stressed and worried and upset, common sense is usually the first thing that flies out the window.

Are you happy with the way your life is going?

If not, you need to change the way you think and that's not as easy to do as it is to say. That's why, sometimes, you need to fake it until you make it!

I decided to write this book partly because I kept getting upset at all the happy-clappy self-help books out there. You know – the ones that tell you to think positive and to feel on top of the world, without telling you how to do it.

From personal experience, I can tell you that when your life's going down the toilet fast, being told to feel positive isn't helpful. The only thing you feel like doing is ripping the head off the person dishing out the free advice!

It also makes you feel like a failure, because the books say being positive is all you have to do to be a success, and it just isn't happening for you.

So, close your eyes and take a deep breath. Now, open your eyes wide and put a huge smile on your face. You will look excited and full of energy. Before you know where you are, you'll feel that way, too.

What you give out, you get back

When you look enthusiastic and full of life, it's catching. People around you get excited and motivated and you start bouncing off each other. Remember they don't know you're only pretending to feel positive, they believe you are feeling positive. When that's coming back at you, your spirits will soar and you'll get the strength to carry on.

When you walk about with a face like fourpence, you bring everyone down with you. So, when you next feel like your life is heading down the Swanee try to look at the situation differently. Imagine all the wonderful things you have to look forward to. Take the time to daydream about what your new life will be like – then go out and live it!

Notes

4

Plan 39

I saw the ad at the job centre in Blackpool and thought it sounded right up my alley, even though they were looking for an experienced photographer. I was sure I could bluff my way through – I was desperate. The job was at Pontins Holiday Camp – an alternative Butlins. They needed another full-time photographer to take pics of the happy campers going about their fun and games. After such a miserable winter it was exactly what I needed, to be surrounded by holidaymakers kicking up their heels and having fun.

I would have said anything to get the job, and I did. When I was shown the camera, I said it was very similar to one I'd used before and that I'd have no problem with it. After being in sales for the last ten years, the one thing I certainly knew how to sell was myself!

Whatever they asked me to do, I assured them nothing would give me more pleasure and asked when I could start. The company were thrilled to have someone so keen and experienced sitting in front of them, so they gave me the job there and then. I started the next day.

I was given my camera and films and spent hours clicking away at the glamorous granny competition, the donkey derby and the tiny tots talent show. The bosses were very pleased that I was always in the right place at the right time, taking hundreds of photographs. They weren't best pleased the next day, however, when the films were developed. My subjects either had their heads cut off, or their legs – sometimes both. Or, if the picture had been framed right, chances are I had the exposure setting wrong and everyone looked like black blobs.

A meeting was called. I had to come clean and admit that I did tell a bit of a porky to get the job and I hadn't actually used any sort of camera at all, ever. But, I made it clear I was very keen to learn – in my own time, of course. I asked them to give me another chance, and agreed to wear a fancy-dress costume at night, to entice more people to have their photographs taken. I wanted that job.

So during the day, when I wasn't taking photos of people swimming, eating or taking part in one of the many competitions, I was in a little booth putting tiny photos in key rings to sell. By night, I had to don a red velvet bunny-girl outfit, complete with fluffy ears and tail. I felt a right idiot, but every night I put on my performance face and sat on the knees of hundreds of strange men. I never asked if they wanted to have their photos taken with me, or if, indeed, I could sit on their knee. As Anna used to say, 'Don't ask a question that can have a negative answer.'

Instead, I'd just plonk myself down and say, 'Smile at the camera,' and they'd smile. The next day in the shop there'd be hundreds of pictures of me all around the walls, and people would come in to see theirs. I looked exactly the same in every photo, every day, smiling from ear to ear as though I'm having a whale of a time. Those photos used to sell out in a few hours. That 'face' came in handy on many occasions and it still does.

Some ladies could get a bit funny about a strange woman sitting on their husband's lap and occasionally they'd have a go at me, so it didn't surprise me one day when a lady stopped to ask if I was the lass in question. I looked a bit different in my ordinary clothes. I said I might be as I thought for a minute she was going to give me a wallop. When she started thanking me profusely, I couldn't think what I might have done to deserve it.

Apparently her husband had been in an accident many years ago and was now in a wheelchair, unable to do anything for himself. He didn't seem aware of anything going on around him and when she spoke to him had never given any indication that he understood. He just sat and stared straight ahead. She couldn't believe her eyes when she saw the photo of us on the shop wall. Not only was I grinning like a Cheshire cat, so was he! She had tears running down her cheeks as she hugged me and so did I. A few months later she wrote to tell me that her husband had smiled several times since then, and there'd been an article published about the whole saga in the *British Medical Journal*. It was shaping up to be quite a summer!

Because I was working such long hours, Pontins let me have one of the guest chalets to live in for the rest of the season to save time travelling back and forth. It also meant I was entitled to all my meals free in the dinner hall – life was getting better and better.

> I was running out the front door screaming my head off before you could say 'stark naked'.

Things did get a bit weird for a while though. In the height of the season the camp hired a new entertainer for the theatre. He was an escapologist and he moved into the chalet next to mine. Part of his act was to lock himself into a small glass cube and have tarantulas crawl all over his body, while he tried to escape. He kept the spiders in his chalet and I used to have nightmares about them escaping and coming into mine.

As things turned out, it was his python, Monty, I should have been worried about! One night when I was soaking in the bath I saw its head start to come through the open window. More and more of the snake slithered in and it was heading straight down into the bath. I don't think I've ever moved so quick in my entire life. I was running out the front door screaming my head off before you could say 'stark naked'. I was greeted by howls of laughter and the sight of Monty's owner holding onto the tail end of his snake, while he pushed him through my bathroom window. I called him for everything then, realising I was dripping wet and naked as a jay bird, ran screaming back inside!

During all the years I spent trekking around England selling my wares, I had the occasional boyfriend but nothing serious. Things would always fizzle out when I had to move on. That summer I fell for a Jack-the-lad gardener by the name of Tommy Murphy. We had a bit of a fling for a couple of months and then he decided he wanted to play the field a bit – and it had nothing to do with gardening.

That was the problem with holiday camps. With hundreds

of single women working there, plus all the others coming and going on their holidays, there was a never-ending supply of tottie. It certainly was not the environment for a long-term relationship. I spent the rest of the season watching him parade a variety of trollops around the bars at night. I used to squirm with embarrassment if I came across them while I was wearing my bunny girl outfit – Tommy would tease me mercilessly.

One day there was great excitement amongst the girls, when a new chef arrived to work in one of the kitchens. Word soon went round about the gorgeous young American with the sexy accent. I was very flattered that night when I was out with a girlfriend and he made a beeline for me. He had all the chat-up lines down pat and he was quite attractive – if you like that sort of thing. Even though he wasn't really my type, we became an item. He was good fun, if a bit intense. If I'm honest, I thought it might make the gardener jealous, as an added bonus.

Brent was always talking about his family 'back home in the States' and showing me photos of the house where he grew up. He pointed out where it was on the map and we talked about going to visit his folks at the end of the season. The other girls were green with envy. I thought all my Christmases had come at once and that I was onto a good thing – I was already dreaming about my new life in California.

I laughed out loud when Brent asked me to marry him. After all, we'd only known each other a couple of months. He got very angry when I told him that I didn't want to rush into things and he started kicking at my chalet door until it came off its hinges.

I thought he was over-reacting somewhat and told him he should be nominated for an Oscar for his performance. I didn't understand when he replied, 'You don't know how right you are.'

I finally understood one night about four months later when I got back to my room to find it had been ransacked. The money I'd saved for my trip to the States had been taken; so had all my gold jewellery, including my gorgeous charm bracelet. Even my tiny portable TV had gone. The police were called and after discovering that Brent Carter Jr was also on the missing list, it became obvious that he'd done a runner with all my stuff and would probably never be seen again.

Tommy Murphy found the whole matter hilarious and would shout after me, 'Any news from the septic tank?' That's rhyming slang for yank. I felt like the laughing stock of the whole camp and I was glad when the season finished.

So, instead of sunning myself in California, I was back in Wolverhampton for another dreary winter – yet more plans down the gurgler. I had a phone call a couple of months later from the fraud squad to say that, thanks to my photograph, they'd caught 'Brent Carter'. It turned out that he was actually a professional conman who wasn't even American. I thought they must have the wrong guy and told them so, but it turned out they'd been after him for a while – he was a bigamist who'd conned his many wives out of houses and life savings all over England. He must have been a bit disappointed with my few bits of jewellery and old black and white telly.

The story got better. Brent Carter wasn't even his real name. I dropped the phone and collapsed with laughter when they told me what it really was. It turned out he was Yorkshire born and bred, and he'd been christened Gary Dennis Bunclark. Sometimes, you just have to see the funny side.

While I was demonstrating at an exhibition I met a magician whose wife had recently become pregnant. She was also his assistant and couldn't fit into the costumes anymore. I was the same size as her and he said I could have her job. Apparently, they'd accepted a season on a cruise ship due to sail in a month's time. I couldn't believe my luck, and gave them my phone number.

I never heard from them again – I was devastated. It had all sounded so wonderful and I couldn't understand why they'd changed their minds. Years later, I bumped into the magician again. He came hurrying over to me and asked why I hadn't returned his call about the cruise.

By all accounts he'd spoken to my stepfather and given him details and a phone number to call. They were annoyed that I hadn't replied. Annoyed didn't begin to describe how I felt. But Bill could be like that. He thought it was funny. Mum and Bill split up not long after that.

As none of my plans were working out in England, I decided to move offshore. The island of Jersey sounded ideal so I found a bed-and-breakfast place I could afford for a couple of weeks and set about finding a job for the summer.

After a few days I came across a stand called 'Pick a Pearl' down a little arcade in the town centre. I watched the girls working and thought I could do just as well, if not better. I had a word with their boss. She said she didn't need any more staff, but when I offered to work a day for nothing, she readily agreed and quickly showed me what to do.

The job entailed getting a crowd assembled, opening an oyster and showing the amazed onlookers the beautiful pearl nestled inside the flesh. There were always gasps of delight – mainly from me – at the wonderful size and lustre of the discovered pearl. Someone always wanted to buy it. The cultured pearls would be

> When I'm desperate for cash, there's no one can out sell me.

set into rings or made into necklaces there and then, and the whole process was repeated again and again.

I loved the job and wanted to show the boss what I was capable of, so I worked like the clappers all day, pulling crowd after crowd, opening oysters left right and centre. She had record takings that day, as I had hoped she would. When I'm desperate for cash, there's no one can outsell me. If you have enough motivation, you can do anything.

So the boss kept me on and even found me somewhere to live. She had several pearl stands all over the island, and I got to work a different site each week. It was one of the nicest jobs I ever did and it was a wonderful summer. I was sorry when it all came to an end.

When I started the job I asked to be put on commission because I expected to sell more than the other girls. It didn't seem fair that we were all paid the same. Plus, I was always the first to arrive in a morning so I used to set up the stands by myself. She told me not to worry. We would all get a bonus at the end that would reflect the amount of work we'd done and the sales we'd achieved.

However, on the last day I was furious when I discovered that, in fact, we all got exactly the same bonus, no matter what. I knew I'd been taken for a ride. The boss even had the nerve to ask me to return again the following year. I told her to shove it where a monkey shoves his nuts. I will not work for people who don't stand by their word – they're not to be trusted.

I headed back to Wolverhampton not knowing what I was going to do next or where I was going. It was time to think about what I really wanted, and to make some new plans. I decided that Australia would be a great place to live. Wasn't it called 'the land of opportunity'? So I got some travel brochures and studied up on it.

There was a world fair – Expo '88 – planned for the following year to commemorate the bicentennial of European settlement of Australia. It was due to open in Brisbane in March and run for six months. I was sure I could get some sort of work there.

I had a few months to try to sort something out. I sent letters out all over the place and eventually got hold of an application form to be a hostess in the British pavilion. Even though they wanted eighteen- to twenty-four-year-olds and I was already thirty-two, I was sure that once they met me they'd realise I was perfect for the job despite my age. I put on my application that I was twenty-five – I had always looked young for my age and I couldn't see that it would make any difference.

While I was waiting to hear back, I started selling a portable steam iron around several department stores. It was a great demonstration and it always drew a big crowd and sold really well. In those days people used to iron everything. If you weren't taking creases out, you were putting them in. Razor sharp creases in jeans were all the rage then!

The iron itself was made out of plastic. I would fill it with water, add a pinch of salt and plug it in. Within a minute, steam would be billowing out, and I would proceed to iron a variety of clothes while they were still on the hanger. The crowd used to go wild. No more standing at the ironing board for hours – the irons used to race out the door.

I was having a great time; it was the perfect product to sell – or so I thought until I started having electric shocks from them. Without warning, every now and then, I'd pick up the iron to steam the creases from a velvet jacket and I'd get a massive electric shock up my arm. It would be so bad that my neck would go rigid, the veins would stand out and my jaw would lock. It would last about three seconds and I would try to keep smiling, hoping the punters hadn't noticed. I didn't want to lose a sale. I became scared of picking the thing up, not only because it was extremely painful but also because I thought the next shock might be worse and my last.

Things all came to a head one day when I noticed smoke coming out of the back of the iron. I tried to finish the demonstration quickly before the thing blew up. Next thing I know, there were flames everywhere. The hanging clothes had caught fire! Instead of running away, my would-be customers stood there watching me beat the fire out. Alarms were going off all over the shop. I managed to get the fire under control and then told my waiting crowd the irons were available in red or black and asked how they would like to pay. I wasn't really surprised when no one bought one. And that was the end of that.

In January 1988 I received a letter from the British government asking me to go to a job interview for work at the Expo '88 pavilion in a few weeks time. The only problem was that the interviews were being held in Brisbane. No matter, I'd been telling everyone for months that I was going to Australia to work in the British pavilion. I really felt I'd already got the job and used to wonder what the uniform would be like. Would I have to wear tights, given how hot it is over there?

My father nearly had a conniption when I told him I was going to Australia for a job interview. He pointed out I didn't have much money to take with me, that I didn't have anywhere to live and that I didn't know anyone when there. He had a point. In fact, he had made three very good points. Anyway, I was so convinced I had the job that off I went to the other side of the world for an interview that went fantastically well. Or so I thought.

PLAN 39

Any plan is better than no plan

Plan 39 was to go to Australia. I always had a plan on the go. My friends used to joke about it, because they always seemed to go wrong.

I would claim that I was just in the wrong place, at the wrong time, usually with the wrong product, and I'd make a new plan. Now I'm so used to doing it that I have several plans on the go at the same time.

A plan gets you moving

It's all very well having dreams and desires, but as soon as you write them down they become goals and plans. I love New Year. I find it exciting to sit down with a journal and make all my new plans for the year.

You don't have to know how you're going to accomplish them at this stage, you're just writing down, what it is you want or what you want to achieve.

Don't think about what's possible and what's not, don't cross something out because you think it's unrealistic, just write down your goals, whatever they are.

I don't just write a list of all the things I want to do and to have. I write down why I want them and what my motivation is. Seeing it written down, in black and white, helps me keep going when I feel like giving up.

You don't have
to do everything,
you just have
to do something.

Goals become plans

Make sure you write down some personal goals, things that you keep saying you're going to do or have always wanted to do. You need to have some fun goals as well as financial ones. Write down if you want to take up rock climbing or ballroom dancing. Maybe you want to lose weight or give up smoking. Instead of being things you just talk about doing, when you write them down they'll start to happen. Your life will be transformed.

BIG PLAN
LITTLE STEPS

A lot of people panic after they've made a plan. It looks impossible to achieve and they don't know how they're going to do it all, so they do nothing.

But you don't have to do everything, you just have to do something. Sir Edmund Hillary climbed Mount Everest one step at a time.

Next to each of my plans, I write down one step I could take, to get things moving. It might be a phone call, an email or looking up something on the internet.

Then I do it. I follow through.

The great thing is, once you've taken that first small step, the next step will become obvious.

For every action there's a reaction

Every single action you take affects your destiny.

Taking the first small step will start a chain reaction of events and get things moving. As you move forward, the second step will become clear, and so on.

Whenever I feel myself starting to panic, thinking the road ahead is too hard and there's too much to do, I remind myself that I only have to take a single step to keep things moving.

Notes

5

What if?

I must admit, I was feeling a bit teary-eyed as I came through customs into the arrivals hall at Brisbane Airport. It seemed as if everyone but me was being met by some long-lost relative. I felt more alone than ever. I saw a boarding house being advertised that was quite cheap, plus they would come to the airport and get me.

My interview was the next day. I had been less than honest about my age on the job application form – I didn't think my age would affect my ability to do the job. But I soon realised

I'd have to come clean when it became obvious they'd need my passport to get me the required working visa.

I blew my own trumpet for all I was worth, but Pamela Hanky, the woman who interviewed me, said they were really looking for university leavers. She said she'd ring me in a few days and let me know if I had the job or not.

Turns out not. I was devastated to receive a phone call a week later to tell me I hadn't got the job. It had never occurred to me that I might not get the job – it wasn't an option. I believed with all my heart that I was going to be working at Expo '88. I'd seen myself wearing the uniform, laughing and chatting with all the other staff. I'd imagined I was showing visitors around the pavilion, extolling the virtues of good old Blighty.

To be told I hadn't got the job took my breath away. My heart started to beat faster and I felt as if I couldn't breathe. I kept thinking I must have heard wrong – I'd seen the future and this wasn't it.

I was in shock for the next three days. I couldn't think what I should do or what I wanted to do. I didn't know whether to look for another job. I didn't have a work visa so no one could legally employ me. Maybe I should call home and tell someone, but they'd ask me what I was going to do next and I didn't know. I only knew I felt like a right idiot. And I cried quite a lot.

To say I was ecstatic when I received a phone call telling me they'd changed their minds is an understatement. I smiled at strangers in the street and shared the fantastic news with anyone who would listen. I was absolutely beside myself. I sent postcards back to friends and relatives and knew they'd all be saying, 'She did it. She got the job.' I couldn't have been happier if I'd won the lottery.

There was a slight hiccup when I found out the job didn't start for another few weeks. Plus, I couldn't change my holiday visa into a work visa while I was in Australia. I had to fly to New Zealand and make the application there. I was going to have to stay a couple of weeks there, until the new visa came through. The problem was, I had enough money for the return airfare but not enough for accommodation. And I would still have to survive until my first pay packet came through once I got back to Australia. Not to worry. I'd come this far and I knew I'd think of something.

I decided to use the money I had left to fly to Auckland, stay at a backpackers and get a job that would pay me cash until my visa came through. It was quite a tall order. There were quite a lot of What Ifs, but I chose not to think about them.

As soon as I was settled into a room in a cheap backpackers' lodge in Auckland, I got the daily newspaper to see if there were any suitable vacancies and, instead, saw an ad for the Royal Easter Show. I set off straightaway to find it. Where there are things to buy, they need people to sell. I walked around asking at stalls if they needed any help. I got dozens of refusals before I came across a very tired looking man trying to flog his metal polish. He said I could mind his stand while he ran a few errands.

When he came back an hour later I'd sold more polish than he had in all the day before. As I said, no one can outsell me when I'm desperate!

I ended up working on the stand every day and George covered the stall when I needed a break. He paid me a commission and I earned enough to move out of the backpackers and stay in a cheap hotel. As soon as my visa came through, I went

> It never occurred to me that I might not get the job — it wasn't an option.

back to Brisbane and began the staff training with the other thirteen members of the British pavilion team.

Pamela Hanky informed us that we were all sensible adults, so she wasn't putting anyone in charge. We would work it out among ourselves when to take a break. If you're under twenty-five that apparently translates to 'let's do bugger all, because there's nobody here to tell us off'. As a result, it was complete chaos in the British pavilion for the first two weeks.

I would watch in disbelief as members of staff disappeared for hours, leaving their posts unattended. Visitors were left to get themselves on and off mechanical rides while six members of staff all went to lunch together. I was running myself ragged trying to stop the mayhem.

It all came to a head one day when Hanky Panky paid us a surprise visit. Out of ten staff rostered on that day, only three of us were at our designated posts. She found four in the pub next door, one young man was asleep under the staffroom table and another was asleep in a cupboard. Then she came across the tenth person in her office having a nice long chat with her mother back in England. Obviously, things had to change. Only one girl got the sack and the others were threatened with it, unless they did as they were told. The three goody-two-shoes that had been taking their jobs seriously were asked to do the telling. We were promoted to supervisor status and the pavilion ran more smoothly after that.

Mostly, the staff were still lazy little sods, but now I could say 'Oi! Get back to work, you lazy little sod,' and they would. It did create a them-and-us work situation, but I tried hard not to be Miss Bossy Boots.

Sometimes for an easy life, I'd do the job myself. One of the jobs was to get in early, open up the pavilion and get everything switched on and running smoothly. Because there was a party to attend nearly every night, the staff could never get up in a morning. Rather than be at home worrying that they might have slept in, to be on the safe side I used to go in anyway.

One morning, with half an hour to opening, I could hear John Farnham singing somewhere outside. I knew he was performing that night on the outdoor stage so I went to investigate. There he was, large as life, rehearsing with his band. I stood right in front of the stage with the cleaning lady and got a private performance. It was one of the most memorable experiences of my entire life. The cleaning lady and I both stared up at him in complete awe and I nearly had a fit when he asked if I had a special request. I still cry now whenever I hear him sing 'Touch of Paradise'.

Working at the British pavilion was a catalyst for my whole life to change. Observing other people's behaviour changed the way I thought about myself. Being raised in a poor working-class area, I always felt intimidated by anyone with a posh accent. If people spoke better than I did, I thought it meant their opinions were better than mine and they knew what they were talking about. I would never have dreamed of saying they were wrong. I felt they were better than me. But that changed.

I found out that some very clever people could still act like complete idiots, and that some members of the Oxbridge brigade could say the stupidest things. Being put in charge of a bunch of smart arses made me realise I wasn't so daft after all. Just because they could remember facts and figures better than I could, didn't make their ideas any better than mine. They just had good memories. That's all. Oh, and university degrees.

I definitely put the 'common' in common sense! A couple of years ago I bumped into one of the guys that worked in the pavilion with me – one of the harder-working lads. He told me that I was right all those years ago, when I told him it was likely to be the best job he'd ever have. I used to tell them all the time how lucky they were. I had the feeling that Ben was longing for the fun-filled days of Expo, now that he was a real estate agent.

After Expo I had a couple of weeks' holiday along the Sunshine Coast and headed for Sydney to look up a long lost aunt – my dad's youngest sister. She'd left England when I was a child and I was keen to tell her all the family gossip. She kindly invited me to stay with her for as long as I liked. I enjoyed a hot Australian Christmas while working in a mall promoting French perfume, before heading back to England and working at the Ideal Home Exhibition.

That year, instead of selling Mista Bright, I worked on the massage pillow stand with some very good friends of mine, who were also excellent demonstrators. Because the massage pillow was quite a bulky product to carry around, people would come back later in the day to buy them. It was impossible to work out who the customer 'belonged' to. Instead of working individually for commission, everybody's sales were split equally between us all at the end of the month. You can only do that if you're all good strong workers, otherwise there's bickering about who's doing all the work and who's swinging the lead.

The massage pillow stand was one of the most popular at the show that year because it was one of the few places you could sit down. After traipsing round for hours, people didn't care that they had to endure the demonstration if they could have a rest for ten minutes and, even better, have a free massage at the same time. We were on the go from when the doors opened to when they closed. It was absolutely exhausting but we were earning good money and I quickly had about half of my airfare back to Australia. I had a new plan to sell massage pillows over there and make a fortune with my own team of girls working the malls. I was telling everyone about the idea at every chance I got – I was so excited.

After the exhibition finished, the company asked me to work several department stores around the country with their newest product – diamond-weight starpoint nine-carat gold-plated jewellery. It was the longest demonstration I've ever had to learn and took a good thirty minutes from start to finish. It had been put together by all sorts of psychologists and marketing experts and they insisted it was done word for word. I had to have an assistant to run around the store first, giving out free raffle tickets. I would call everyone on my microphone to come over as I was about to draw the raffle any minute. I even had Mum be my assistant for a week in Skegness. She'd separated from my stepfather by then, and was looking after young Billy by herself. She was always in need of some extra cash.

The whole idea of the demonstration was to gather a huge crowd, and keep them there, by promising to do the raffle any second – 'But just let me show you this lovely necklace first.' It was all about reverse psychology. After repeatedly telling the waiting crowd that they couldn't buy the jewellery because it wasn't for sale, of course everyone wanted to buy it! So, I would agree to sell them entire sets of diamond-weight starpoint nine-carat gold-plated jewellery for a very special price and then, finally, I would draw the raffle.

It worked every time and before long I had the airfare back to Australia.

The ticket I bought gave me a free week-long stopover in Auckland. After a good explore of the city, I decided that I didn't feel as lost and insignificant as I had in Sydney. Plus, I had a feeling that because New Zealand was a bit behind the times there would be more opportunity for me to shine. I decided to stay.

> No matter how many jobs I had on the go, I couldn't seem to make ends meet.

I couldn't find any demonstrating work but got a job in a dry-cleaners shop. In those days the city was closed for the weekend. I thought it was very quaint and it was the first time in all of my working life that I'd had a Saturday off. Monday to Friday in the dry-cleaners didn't pay much, so I also got a weekend job at a café in Victoria Park Market, a popular tourist destination. I also worked two or three nights a week as a waitress at Burgundys nightclub in Parnell and I put my name down with a large catering company. I was regularly called upon to work in the private boxes at rugby games and cricket matches and served in a corporate-hospitality tent at the 1990 Commonwealth Games. I preferred to work than sit in an apartment by myself.

I couldn't believe my luck when I saw they were advertising for hostesses to entertain businessmen. I had a fantastic reference from the British government from my time as a hostess in the pavilion at Expo '88. I thought there wouldn't be many young women with that sort of recommendation.

The interview was held in a fabulous waterfront apartment in Herne Bay. I was interviewed by an attractive well-groomed woman in her forties. She told me I'd have to escort out-of-town businessmen to dinner and meetings, and asked how I was at small-talk and socialising. I thought it was right up my street and was keen to start work right away. She showed me a huge wardrobe with a vast array of evening dresses, business suits, handbags and shoes. I could borrow anything if I didn't have suitable outfits to wear. Plus, the money I could make was incredible. It sounded like a dream job to me. I'd definitely fallen on my feet here.

When she said it was up to me if I took a shower afterwards or not, I wondered how she thought I was going to get myself dirty. I understood, finally, when she advised me to always use protection and to keep something in my handbag. I was mortified when the penny dropped – I'd nearly become a hooker! I was so embarrassed that I couldn't get out of there quick enough. My flatmate thought it was hilarious and couldn't believe I'd been so naïve. I couldn't believe I'd been so stupid.

I did manage to get a job in promotions and left the dry-cleaners to work for the tobacco company, Marlboro. I had to wear an all-in-one, red-and-white jumpsuit and stand around dairies asking customers if they smoked. If they did I'd offer them a free Marlboro Lite. Apparently they made you cough less than other cigarettes.

The part I liked best was going along to the races that Marlboro sponsored to wave the starting flag. It was pretty exciting and I got to travel around New Zealand a bit. I fell completely in love with the country and the people and I'd already decided I wanted to make it my permanent home.

Unfortunately, my attempts to bring the massage pillow to New Zealand had been unsuccessful. The companies I'd been dealing with in England thought the country was too small to bother – the population then was about three million.

But no matter how many jobs I had on the go, I couldn't seem to make ends meet. Public transport was virtually non-existent and I seemed to spend all my time and money getting from A to B. The exchange rate was dreadful and any money I sent back home to help out turned into pennies. I couldn't seem to get on top of things and my visa was running out – I had no choice but to return to Wolverhampton.

I was thirty-five years old, with no money, no home, no husband or children. No car, nothing. A wave of sadness washed over me when someone joked, 'Never mind. At least you've got two suitcases full of clothes. You always look good while you're failing.' For the first time in my adult life, I felt like a failure.

Most of my friends had husbands, children and their own homes. I'd been working for twenty years, chasing my dreams all over the world. I'd made plan after plan, but I had nothing to show for it.

Losing the dream of having things can be as painful as if you really have lost them. I mourned the loss of the life I thought I was going to have.

I felt I'd let Mum and Billy down. I'd promised to get them out of the council slums they were living in. Instead, I was back there living with them. I felt like I'd fallen into a big black hole and I couldn't see any way out. There didn't seem much point in making any new plans; I didn't want to do anything. I felt completely worn out. And I felt foolish, too. Thank goodness for my friend Kathy, who saved me.

Fate, destiny or good luck?

It never occurred to me that I wouldn't get the job at Expo; I'd wanted it so badly that I'd thought of little else, every day for months.

It didn't cross my mind to make an alternative plan – I was so convinced I had the job. But as it turned out, if I had made other arrangements I would have been long gone from the boarding house when the second call came through to say the job was mine.

Ask and you shall receive

I always get a car park right where I want it. As I drive to my destination, I'm thinking about where I'm going to park when I get there. If I'm going to the supermarket, I imagine that I'll be parking right outside the front door, near the trolley park. I don't doubt it. I tell everyone how lucky I am that I always find a great parking space.

I don't know how it happens, I just know that it does.

Sometimes, you have to believe in something one hundred per cent – you have to know, without a shadow of a doubt, that what you have set your heart on will happen.

There is great power in absolute, total belief.

If I'd thought for one minute that I wouldn't get the job in Australia, I would never have left Wolverhampton.

If you do what
you've always done,
you'll get what
you've always got.

Don't play the 'What If?' game

What if I had a dollar for every time someone said 'What if?' to me?

What if you can't find anywhere to live?

What if you don't get the job?

What if you run out of money?

CREATE YOUR OWN DESTINY

Some people can 'What if?' themselves right out of doing anything!

What if I make a fool of myself?

What if I fail?

What if I make the wrong decision?

As soon as you start having these conversations with yourself, just stop.

If you don't, you'll never get to try anything different. You'll be stuck in the same old rut, doing the same old things.

And if you do what you've always done, you'll get what you've always got.

Notes

The big picture

During the next couple of miserable months, I seemed to hear the words 'I told you' over and over again. I could feel my blood boiling and the anger welling up every time. 'I told you to spend the money on a car, not flit off to the other side of the world.' 'I told you to put your name down for a council house. Now there's a twelve-year waiting list.' 'I told you to get married and settle down.' 'I told you so.'

Those three words should be banned from the English language. Every time I heard them, I could feel myself sinking further and further down. I felt everyone else was right and I was wrong, and I'd been wrong about everything.

I was thirty-five years old and had no idea what the hell I was doing. I was lonely and I was frightened.

My friend Kathy kept asking me about my new plan. When I didn't come up with one, she invited me to go and stay with her in Sunderland up in the North of England, just south of the Scottish border. She lived with her husband and two-year-old daughter on a council estate. At least it would be a change of scenery and a fresh start. The house was a two-up two-down in a rough neighbourhood. Kathy's husband worked down the mines with most of the other men in town. A lot of the pits had been closed down during the Margaret Thatcher years and there was a huge unemployment problem in the area. I was lucky to find a job promoting fitted kitchens outside a supermarket. There was a roof overhead but no side walls, and the wind went right through me. It was the middle of winter and I looked like Nanook of the North standing there with so many clothes on I couldn't bend my arms!

I had a kitchen cupboard display and a clipboard to write down the names and addresses of anyone interested in being measured for new units. Thank God I was getting a basic wage and not just earning commission. I don't think I've ever been so bored in my entire life, standing there hour after hour, day after day. I thought I'd go round the bend.

> I was thirty-five years old and I had no idea what the hell I was doing. I was lonely and I was frightened.

Instead, I started thinking about New Zealand and the sort of life I wanted for myself and I started to write it all down on my clipboard.

Every day the plan got bigger and more detailed, right down to the layout of the house I was going to build, the type of car I was going to buy and the colour of it. I looked at that plan every day and told Kathy about it every night, until she was sick of hearing about it. 'When you going to En Zed, then?' she joked.

When I landed the swyng brush demonstration in a department store I started earning good money again. Plus, it was indoors and out of the weather and I felt as if things were looking up again. The swyng brush was a hairbrush aimed at the older woman with short curly or permed hair, which was a popular style at the time. The ladies used to come in by the bus load. I'd run the brush over their heads and it would make the flat curls spring up again. All the old dears loved it and I moved from town to town, brushing and styling as fast as I could go.

After several months I had enough saved for the airfare back to New Zealand and I went home for a few weeks to tidy up some loose ends and say goodbye to everyone. Then the What Ifs started up again. I toyed with the idea of spending the money on a car instead of a plane ticket – after five attempts I'd finally passed my driving test. If I had a car I could get a good job as a sales rep.

I'd talk myself first one way, then the other. I was torn with indecision.

Then a funny thing happened that helped me make up my mind once and for all. My mum asked my brother and me if we would go with her up to the local pub to see some psychics perform. We both agreed to, as long as she was buying the drinks. The pub was just around the corner from where we lived so we'd always recognise a few faces. That night there were four psychics on a small stage and great excitement in the bar. The psychics took it in turns to yell out things at the audience –

'Does anyone know a Harry?' 'Has anyone lost an Edna?' Billy and I thought the whole thing was a great laugh and I joked, 'The only spirits in here are behind the bar!'

We both went quiet when we realised people were pointing at us, saying, 'She's talking to you.' From up on the stage one of the psychics said, 'Yes, I've got a message for you in the blue top. You're thinking about going overseas on a long journey and you don't know whether to go because you've been before and it didn't work out.' Spot on so far, and my mouth was hanging open in astonishment as she continued, 'But I have to tell you that you must go. This time, you only have to buy a one-way ticket. You won't be coming back because you're going to make piles and piles of money!'

As far as I was concerned, that was it. I went and bought a one-way ticket to New Zealand the next day.

While I was demonstrating the swyng brush, I'd mentioned to my boss that I was going to Auckland pretty soon to live. She said it was a coincidence because she'd just got back from there and she gave me the phone number of a man she thought was a bit of an entrepreneur. She suggested I give him a call.

I'd paid some bills and settled a few debts and when the plane touched down in Auckland I had the princely sum of eighteen dollars to my name, but I wasn't too worried. It's amazing the jobs you can find when you've got no money.

An English girl I knew from my first visit picked me up from the airport and I went to stay with her in Beach Haven on Auckland's North Shore. I had to get a job straightaway and, after scanning the newspaper, I fixed myself up with an interview the very next day. I got the job, which wasn't down to anything clever or witty I said in the interview. Everyone who turned up was offered the same job.

I did two days of staff training before I was ready to go out selling Kirby vacuum cleaners door to door. It was the dirtiest, filthiest, smelliest, most disgusting job I've ever had, and I had to remind myself that it was just a means to an end. Not only did I vacuum people's floors and furniture, but I used to strip their beds to suck up bed fleas and dust mites – I had photos to prove they were in there! By the time I got home at night, my skin was crawling and itching, and even after a hot shower I'd still be scratching. I'm scratching now just thinking about it, but Kirby was the Rolls-Royce of vacuum cleaners and very expensive. I only had to sell a couple to earn some good commission and then I'd be out of there.

I also rang the number I'd been given by my boss back in England saying, 'You don't know me, but I can sell anything. If you've got something I can sell, we'll both make a lot of money.' We arranged to meet outside McDonald's in the city. There were two guys waiting to meet me when I arrived and, over a burger, I showed them the vibrating massage pillow. They were keen to get some made and I gave them my phone number.

I was also doing one-off jobs at various exhibitions, promoting different products and services. One of these was SKY TV, which hadn't been going long. I was one of six girls and we had to stop people and sign them up for it. I've employed a lot of promotions girls over the years and the problem is a that lot of the time they get paid a good wage just to stand about and look good. There's really no incentive for them to lift a finger, so they don't generally bother.

After so many years of not getting paid if I didn't sell anything, I was used to making as many sales as possible. I get bored standing about gossiping. So, as usual, I went like the clappers all day signing up record numbers of people. I didn't get any extra money but I got huge job satisfaction, which is nearly as good. What was even better, a couple of weeks later I had a phone call from a man who had seen me on the SKY stand and had managed to track me down.

'You were like a madwoman compared to the other girls,' he said. 'You just kept going and going. I need somebody to sell sunglasses for me at a pharmacy in Newmarket. Do you want to come and work for me?'

Selling eyewear in a shop sounded a lot nicer than knocking on people's doors and getting covered in dust and fleas so I accepted. It's funny how things work out. Years later that same guy who gave me the job came to work for me at Prestige Marketing as my marketing manager in Australia – I never forget a good turn.

About three months after I started flogging sunglasses, I got a phone call from Paul Meier – one of the guys I'd met at McDonald's. He had some good news. The massage pillows were ready and he wanted to know where I was going to sell them. I was on my way!

After ringing around, I got a spot selling the pillows at what was then Henderson Square shopping mall, on the west side of Auckland city.

I was used to catching trains and buses in England to get to work, and thought the train ride west might be quite nice and probably the fastest way to get there. I called the station to find out the times. Apparently, I would have to get a bus to the city and then catch the 7 am train to Henderson. That seemed a bit too early and I decided to go on the next one, until I found out that was the following day – also at 7 am! The Auckland public-transport system wasn't much to write home about.

In the end, I caught two buses each way and it used to take me nearly two-and-a-half hours to get there and a bit longer to get home at night. But I didn't care, because Kiwis loved the vibrating pillow as much as the Poms and they were flying out the door. I was earning good commission and things got even better when Paul hired a few more girls to work in various malls around the city. I trained them up and then got a small slice of whatever they sold. I was saving every penny I got.

After Christmas we hit the road. We travelled the country demonstrating in shopping malls and at exhibitions and A&P Shows. I started thinking about all the other things I'd sold in England over the years. I figured if the massage pillow had taken off here, there was no reason the other products wouldn't take off, too. Within a few months the girls and I were also demonstrating Mista Clear, which was a polish similar to the old Mista Bright and, once again, we were onto a winner.

Both products were now going great guns, so I had a word with Paul about a make-up that I'd sold in the early eighties. He knew all about it, as his girlfriend was also using it at the time. We approached a cosmetics factory to make it for us, but I wanted to change the formula so it wasn't as dark. The original was also quite glittery and I felt a softer more subtle look would be better for the New Zealand market.

One day after I'd finished work at the Downtown shopping mall I went for a bite to eat and noticed a small-framed foreign-looking gentleman giving me the eye. I saw him again when I came out of the post office and then several more times as I wandered along Queen Street. I was starting to get a bit nervous as I realised I was being followed, when he came right up to me and said, in a delicious French accent, that I had the most beautiful legs he had ever seen. Then he asked if I would have dinner with him! His English was passable and he was very charming and well dressed so I couldn't think of a reason why not.

I'd never been picked up off the street before but my flatmate assured me that dentists were usually very well educated and reliable. After a few dates Mony and I became a couple. He owned a lovely apartment in the city, with beautiful furnishings he'd brought over from Paris, and gorgeous cream carpet everywhere. Around this time a new make-up sample would arrive each week for me to try. The only way I could tell if it was suitable was to wear it for the day and see how it looked and how it lasted on the skin. Problem was, the stuff went everywhere – there was hardly a white towel left in the place and every room had dreadful brown marks on the carpet where the glittery brown powder had spilt. The Frenchman wasn't best pleased to say the least!

I needed to get other people's comments on how I looked wearing the various concoctions and some days I must have looked a right state when I left his apartment. One dark winter's morning I dusted the latest sample on my face thinking I didn't look half bad, but when I got to work I realised I was getting some funny stares. Eventually a work colleague said, 'What's the matter with your face? You look like a red Indian!' I had to go and scrub it all off in the loo. And so it went on for months. I'd alternate between looking orange, red or glittery and, on less fortunate occasions, streaky, patchy and glowing in the dark!

Eventually, the Auckland-based company we had contracted to make the powder got the formula exactly how I wanted it. Although I had been getting mixed reactions from friends and workmates – the majority thought it was too shimmery and that I should go for a matte look –I decided to go with my instinct. I was convinced that once women got used to the fresh natural look they'd love it. I came up with the name Natural Glow.

I didn't know it then, but it was set to become one of the biggest-selling make-ups New Zealand had ever seen and it would turn me into a household name.

Afraid of the future?

There were some days when I was gripped by fear and panic, my heart would start to race and I'd feel like I couldn't breathe. I'd keep going over all the past failures in my mind, replaying everything I could have done differently. I'd worry about the future and how I was going to end up. What was to become of me? I felt completely overwhelmed.

For the first time in my life I was too scared to make a new plan. I was afraid to fail again. I didn't think I'd be strong enough to carry on.

I was afraid to get excited about anything, in case it didn't work out.

When your get up and go has got up and gone

When you feel so low and don't have the energy left to pick yourself up, make sure you only talk with positive, strong people who know you and believe in you. Don't share your fears or your new plans with negative What-Iffers – they'll just bring you down. A real friend will support you.

'A friend hears the song in my heart, and sings it to me when my memory fails.' I think I read that on a birthday card.

**WHEN OPPORTUNITY COMES KNOCKING
DON'T COMPLAIN ABOUT THE NOISE!**

When things
get really bad,
you need to focus
on the big picture.

Was it an amazing coincidence that someone in England gave me Paul Meier's phone number?

Was it a lucky guess for the psychic when she said I only had to buy a one-way ticket?

You have to keep your eyes and ears open to the opportunities when they come your way. I always think that someone up there knows what they're doing and they'll show me the way to go if I look out for the signs.

My husband Duncan has a theory that if we see something or someone out of the blue three times then it's for a reason, and we have to look for it.

The big picture

I'd always looked at life from my salesperson point-of-view – the more nos you get, the closer you are to getting a yes. It is the Law of Average.

For years, I'd been telling people I'd just been in the wrong place at the wrong time. Doesn't the same Law of Averages mean that eventually I will be in the right place at the right time?

The only thing that got me moving forward again was making a plan and believing that I could make it happen. I didn't know how. I just knew that if I started heading in the right direction, what to do next would become obvious.

When things get really bad, you need to focus on the big picture.

When I was standing outside in the snow selling kitchens and vacuuming people's beds, it was the image in my head of how much better my life was going to be that kept me going.

I wouldn't have carried on if I'd thought it was just to pay the bills, or save for my retirement. It would have all seemed too hard and the road ahead too long.

Whenever I feel like giving up, keeping the bigger picture always in my mind gives me the strength to keep going.

Notes

7

Daydream believer

While the Natural Glow was being made I also launched a specially designed scarf clip – the Suzanne clip – that you could do amazing things with. The girls and I had great fun demonstrating it all over the country. The more we did the demonstration the quicker we got, and the ladies would gasp as they witnessed fingers moving like lightning, folding and twisting scarves into dozens of different styles. It was one of my favourite demonstrations and I can still do the Dutch bonnet to this day. We used to do a buy-one-and-get-another-one-absolutely-free offer, which meant you could attach them to your shoes, for a bit of glamour. Needless to say, wherever we went they always sold well.

The name for the scarf clip came about because of the way Mony pronounced my name. I was actually christened Susan but I thought it sounded posher and a bit sexy the way he said it, and so the 'Suzanne clip' was born!

Over the next few months, things changed dramatically. Both Paul and I split up with our partners and started spending more time together. He'd bought an old white van and we travelled all over the country with our various products. Paul was also an excellent salesman and he and his business partner, Michael, used to demonstrate car polish by pouring lighter fuel over a car bonnet and setting fire to it. As you can imagine they used to get huge crowds and cause a great commotion.

Paul and I had similar ambitions and it was nice to finally have someone to talk to who was on the same wavelength. We started having dinner together after the shows and one thing led to another. Within a few months we were living together in a flat attached to his mum's house in Herne Bay. We both lived and breathed work – work was all we did. It was all we talked about. We had a shared goal – to make lots of money in a short space of time.

As soon as the make-up was ready the girls and I started demonstrating it around the country. It was in a big blue pot with *Natural Glow by Etoile de Paris* on the front. Mony had suggested that it would sell better than *Natural Glow by Innovative Marketing*. Whatever the reason, women bought it by the bucket load and we couldn't make it quick enough. They loved it so much they wanted to know where they could buy some more when it ran out, and weren't very satisfied with our answers.

'It might be at the Easter Show' and 'We may have a stand

DAYDREAM BELIEVER

at the Home Show' didn't quite cut the mustard. I talked to Paul about getting pharmacies to stock Natural Glow as I'd also become fed up with my gypsy lifestyle and didn't want to be flitting all over the place anymore, living out of a suitcase. I'd been doing that for nearly twenty years. It was time to stop!

I didn't know how you went about getting a product into the pharmacies. I thought it was just a matter of walking through the door, having a chat to the person in charge and away you go. I was very naïve. I visited dozens of pharmacists all over the city and even offered to stand outside the front of their stores demonstrating Natural Glow for a day, so they could see how well the product sold. I offered to send customers inside to pay so that, at the end of the day, the pharmacy would only pay me wholesale for what had already been sold. They would have made a tidy profit for next to no effort. I couldn't believe it when they all kept saying no.

I started to think maybe they didn't understand what I meant. It was such a good deal for them. Why did they keep turning me down?

I'd try saying it in a different way, but no one wanted to know about Natural Glow. It was so frustrating. I rang Paul one day in tears after a pharmacist grabbed hold of me by my arm, dragged me out the door and said, 'Get out of my shop, motor mouth!'

Finally, after weeks of disappointment, I managed to get Natural Glow in two pharmacies, one in St Lukes mall and the other in Devonport. It was hardly going to make us rich, but it was a start.

Paul came up with the idea of advertising Natural Glow on television to create a demand for it in the pharmacies, while making it available to buy straightaway using an 0800 number. It reminded me of a guy from the Ideal Home Show in England by the name of Johnny Parkin, who'd gone to the States to sell products off TV. There were plenty of rumours about that he'd made a fortune, so we decided to give it a go.

We agreed I'd write the ad based on my mall demonstration and then get Jude Dobson or Lana Coc-Kroft to front it – they were both on TV at the time and very popular. I found I couldn't fit all the information into one ad and ended up writing two separate two-minute commercials. In the end, we discovered we couldn't afford either of these women or, in fact, anyone else. I'd just have to front the ads myself.

When I look back at those first ads I wonder how we sold anything at all – I was so terrified I look as if I'm going to the electric chair. For the shoot, I convinced Paul's sister and a couple of my demonstrators to be models. There was no budget for a hair stylist or make-up artist, so it came down to me to make us all look good. I did our hair and make-up, then loaned the others a dress from my wardrobe. I was so nervous I kept throwing up. Also, I hadn't taken into account the studio lights, which were so hot the sweat was soon pouring off me.

Even though I knew the script word for word I'd never done any filming before, and I felt completely out of my depth. Plus, I didn't want to let Paul down and lose him his money. The ads took all day to film and I was glad when it was over. I felt like the wreck of the *Esprey*, and looked like it, too!

The following day had been set aside for editing so Paul and I went back to the studio to be met with devastating news. There had been a technical hitch and the equipment hadn't recorded any sound. It meant we'd have to film the whole lot again. I just about cried.

The only way we could save the ads was if I would do a voice-over, but it would need to match the timing perfectly. The technicians told me it was virtually impossible – they said I'd look all out of sync. What they didn't know was that I'd spent the last fortnight doing nothing but saying the ads over and over again for hours on end so that they each fitted perfectly into two minutes. When the ads went to air you couldn't tell that they'd been voiced over.

Even so, they were still pretty dreadful. When Paul's business partner saw them he looked absolutely mortified. He thought we all looked shiny and sweaty and that my English accent would put people off. He had a point. He also thought that at $29.95 Natural Glow was too expensive. I strongly disagreed and as we couldn't afford to make another ad, Paul and I decided it should go to air – it had to be better than nothing.

We couldn't settle our 'creative differences' with Michael and Paul's the kind of guy that likes to do things his way. In fact, his motto is, 'It's my way or the highway'. Years later our marketing team had it engraved on a mug for him! It meant Michael had to buy Paul out, or vice versa. It was agreed Michael would come up with a price and if Paul couldn't pay it Michael would have to pay that amount to Paul – and he'd get the company, including Natural Glow.

I don't think I slept for a week. Paul had already put most of his money into stock and production costs, so there wasn't much spare cash. Plus, we didn't have a clue what figure Michael was going to come up with. In the end, even with Paul borrowing a substantial amount, he was still short. He asked me if I had any money I could get my hands on.

Over the last year I'd been trying to save most of my wages. I'd hoped to use it as a deposit on an apartment. I had about eleven thousand dollars in the bank. For me, that was pretty good – I'd never had that sort of money before. I liked the feeling of security it gave me. I'd never had security before either. Paul said if I gave the money to him, instead of working for commission,

I would own twenty per cent of the company.

It was very tempting, but what if the ads didn't work and we lost all our money? What if I was wrong again and ended up back in Wolverhampton broke and desperate? I couldn't bear the thought of that and was frightened of making the wrong decision.

However, I trusted Paul. He was honest and hardworking and a great businessman. When he said he'd do something, he always did it. He was good to his word. He said he'd get me the massage pillows and he had and he was always kind to the girls. He would help them out if they needed money.

I thought about it overnight and decided the expression 'Put your money where your mouth is' was very apt on this occasion. The next day, I bought twenty per cent of a company we called Prestige Marketing. It was the best decision I could have made, and probably the worst one for Michael.

I'll never forget the day that first ad went to air. We were renting a small office and had extra phone lines put in and a TV so we would know when the ads were run. We weren't sure what to expect, but we knew if the ad worked we would need some help answering the calls. Paul's family were there to man the phones and we all stood nervously watching the little TV in the corner. Thank God I was wearing my Natural Glow, or else I'd have been as white as a sheet!

We weren't computerised – we all had a pen and some paper – and I cringed as I heard my own voice screeching out from the TV. You could have cut my accent with a knife, as well as the atmosphere when the ad had finished. The silence was deafening.

It was the longest minute of my life. It was long enough for me to start thinking, 'Please, God, don't make me go back to Wolverhampton. Please let it be my turn.'

DAYDREAM BELIEVER

I nearly jumped out of my slingbacks when all six phones started ringing at once. I was so excited I danced around doing a silly jig until I remembered I was supposed to be answering the phones not doing cartwheels round the room. It was one of the best days of my life.

In the ad, I had stated that Natural Glow was available at selected pharmacies. This was true – it was available in two! That's very select.

As the ad began to appear on TV several times a day, we started to get calls from pharmacies asking if they could stock it – women were going in asking for Natural Glow. It gave me great pleasure telling the pharmacist who called me motor mouth that we wouldn't be supplying him. Childish of me, I know, but it still felt great!

Around this time a new TV show called *Good Morning* started. You could buy a four-minute advertorial slot and I began to make regular appearances. I tried the vibrating massage pillow on the show and it sold just as well as it did in the malls. So I also filmed a two-minute commercial, which proved hugely successful, and all the pharmacies stocked the pillow as well. We were going great guns.

We had a bit of a glitch with the Suzanne clip. We had a bit more money in the bank by then and I decided to do a much more up-market ad with lovely models floating in and out wearing gorgeous scarves clipped every which way.

The ad bombed. I couldn't understand why. I knew the product was a great seller, so there had to be something wrong with the ad. I refilmed it in my usual style – with me standing behind a trestle table doing the demonstration – and the phones nearly rang off the wall! It didn't matter whether people loved my funny British accent or hated it, just as long as they remembered the ads and bought the products. That was all I cared about.

A friend of mine from Wolverhampton came to stay for a while. Vicki was also a top demonstrator and over the years we'd worked many exhibitions together. Other girls had a hard time matching her sales figures. I was thrilled when she decided to settle in New Zealand as I'd been missing my friends and family. We were looking forward to doing lots of girly things together.

But fate had something else in store for Vicki when she met and fell in love with Paul's brother from Australia, Alan, while he was paying us a visit. Within a couple of months she'd gone to live with him in Sydney and went on to marry him. They have two beautiful daughters that I adore. You never know what's round the corner do you?

I didn't have time anymore to work in the malls – I was too busy writing, filming or editing commercials. None of us had time to answer the phones, so we employed a few telephone operators, and we didn't have computers – the orders were still being scribbled on pieces of paper.

Things went well until every customer who had ordered Natural Glow received coloured car polish instead. I had to laugh as we called dozens of women to make sure they didn't try to put the stuff on their faces. They certainly would have got a lovely finish! After that, we realised we were growing bigger and bigger every month and really needed someone to oversee the day-to-day running of the office. We also needed to get computerised.

We took on an incredible office manager called Christine and within a few months had moved to bigger premises. Paul and I were able to buy a beautiful ground-floor apartment in St Heliers and I thought I was going to burst with happiness when Paul came to help me choose a gorgeous red convertible sports car. At last, all my dreams were coming true. I'd made it.

As you imagine, you create

Years later, looking back upon this time I realised what a tremendous amount of time and effort I put into creating the life I wanted. It was all I ever thought about and talked about. I focused my entire energies on my success without distractions. I wasn't interested in going out, doing lunch or going shopping. I didn't want to stop because I was on a roll. I thought my luck had changed. What you focus on becomes true.

I've since discovered that this can also work in a negative way. If you keep focusing on bad things or bad times, you draw more of the same towards you. Again, it's the Law of Attraction.

If you focus on failure you'll feel like a failure and things will go from bad to worse.

Whatever you consistently focus on, you'll move towards.

The dynamic duo

No wonder Paul and I were so successful in such a short space of time. We were both continually putting all of our energies into building a multi-million-dollar marketing company.

Double the intensity and positive focus had double the positive attraction.

Blind faith

When I made my wish list, I had no idea how I was going to achieve all the things on it. I kept visualising them anyway. It made me feel good because I really believed I was going to make my dreams come true.

It was blind faith, but what in? Some people put their faith in God and pray for their needs to be met, while others believe aliens make their life fulfilling. I don't think it matters, as long as you truly believe in something. Ask and you shall receive.

I believe somebody up there knows what they're doing.

I believe that the universe wants me to be happy and will give me what I truly believe I should have. I'd seen myself so many times driving that red sports car. It was always in back of my mind and when I bought that convertible for cash, it felt as good as I always imagined it would.

Believing is feeling

It's no good just writing your wish list and then reading it now and then. You need to think about what you want and how you want your life to be every day, even if it's just for a few minutes. You need to have that image of driving your dream car in your mind – you need to smell the new leather and feel the wind in your hair as you drive along. You will feel good because people are admiring it.

That's when magic starts to happen. You're no longer angry because you're driving a clapped-out old banger – you're excited because you know your new car is on the way!

Believe it with all your heart and you will feel the joy.

WORRY IS A WASTED EMOTION

Believing gives you boundless energy and enthusiasm. You feel powerful and strong and, no matter what problems occur, you can work through them. Believing keeps you surging ahead because you know, without a shadow of a doubt, that whatever you've set your mind to will happen – so you don't have anything to worry about.

Think about what you
want and how you
want your life to be
every day.

Notes

8

Passion & perseverance

No one could have imagined what was going to happen next and how my life would suddenly veer off in a different direction. It seemed as if things couldn't get any better. I loved our apartment – I'd never lived anywhere as beautiful before. It even had two bathrooms, and one of them had a spa bath! I thought I was the bee's knees.

My brother Bill came over to stay with us and became our graphic designer. He'd always been great at art and Paul paid for him to learn how to design using the computer. He did the logos and artwork for all our products and was kept pretty busy. We always had something new to launch – they were exciting times and the atmosphere was electric.

We had the best Christmas ever when I flew Mum over for a few weeks' holiday. I'd bought two Persian kittens – known as the girls – and I felt that I belonged somewhere at last. For the first time in my life I felt safe and secure. I could pay the bills. I could save money to treat my family. All the years of stress and worry seemed far behind me and I felt as if a huge weight had been lifted from my shoulders. Life was good.

Natural Glow was flying out the door, but we decided to have a new name on the pot. We'd gone off the French one that my ex had come up with. We wanted a name along the lines of Elizabeth Arden or Estée Lauder. It was Paul who suggested we put both our first names together to make Susan Paul. I didn't think it sounded very glamorous so we went with the French version of my name, same as we had for the scarf clip. 'Natural Glow by Suzanne Paul' was launched onto the market, with its thousands of luminous spheres. What a huge effect it went on to have in my life!

Everywhere I went people were recognising me. I thought it was hilarious – no one in England became famous doing TV ads. I'd never expected to become so well known. I seemed to be the talk of the washhouse. There was a popular comedy show on at the time, called *More Issues*, and every week a woman used to dress up as me, complete with shoulder pads and a French pleat. She'd take the mickey out of me something rotten. She'd try to do my strange accent and talked about radioactive spheres and having a Suzanne clip around the ear. I used to record every episode and send them over to England. My friends and family couldn't believe I was so famous that I was being impersonated! I didn't care if people laughed at me, just as long as they kept buying my products.

It was when the gay community took a shine to me that my profile really shot up. They thought my ads were very camp and I got invited to appear and perform at various gay venues around the country. I'd look like a midget up on stage miming along with Buckwheat and Bertha – a couple of huge drag queens. Sometimes, I'd do a tap dance or a send up of my ads and they loved it.

I'll never forget the time I was in Christchurch as compère for the Drag Queen of the Year awards and six hunky, barely dressed boys carried me through the crowd in a huge replica Natural Glow pot, while I threw out handfuls of luminous spheres – glitter. Just as we got to the stage, the bottom fell out of the pot and I crashed to the floor, cutting my leg open on the way down. Poor Miss Mole was beside herself, but the show must go on, and I stood the rest of the night with blood running down my shin and all over the floor!

The drag queens started introducing me as Suzanne Paul. I'd keep saying, 'No. That's not my name. I'm Susan Barnes,' but the newspapers and magazines also started referring to me as Suzanne Paul and, in the end, that's who I became. Now it's how I think of myself. I certainly don't feel like the scruffy and common Susan Barnes anymore. Later on, I changed my first name by deed poll to Suzanne and everyone calls me that now, except my mum, who still calls me Sue.

Prestige Marketing started working with several overseas companies that were in the same business. We would licence their products and they would supply us with finished ads ready to screen. Commercials were even longer by then and in addition to our usual two-minute ads we started playing thirty-minute infomercials, mainly in the middle of the night because it was cheaper. In those early years, some of our most successful

> *Business was booming. Paul and I would work all day, then talk about work all night.*

products were Blu Blocker Sunglasses, Ginsu knives and a hand-held blender. Every week we received more new products to advertise.

About a year after we started Prestige Marketing, Alan Meier, Paul's brother, set up a similar operation in Sydney. He launched all the products that we had, including the Natural Glow which went into pharmacies right across Australia. My friend Vicki was in charge of the demonstrators, and I'd fly over once a month to appear on the *Good Morning Australia* show with Bert Newton. Sometimes we filmed five or six segments one after the other. Paul and I owned fifty per cent of the Australian company and Alan owned the rest. During one of our get-togethers, Vicki and I shared a bottle of duty-free port. By the end of that night, we had hatched a plan for me to launch a single called 'The Blue Monkey' and I'd give away free videos of how to do the blue monkey dance. It was quite a catchy tune that went something like, 'Get down, get funky, everybody do the blue monkey'.

It was filmed at the Staircase – a gay nightclub. It managed to get into the music charts and the video was often played on the music channel, but I haven't drank port since.

We were also busy writing and filming our own ads for products such as the Florazanne – a flower-arranging-by-numbers contraption that I invented, the Easy Vee (vase), and the Penalli (pen set).

Business was booming. Paul and I would work all day, then talk about work all night until, after three years, we realised we didn't have anything else in common and had drifted apart.

I felt very sad when we split up. By then, my brother Bill had gone over to work in our Sydney office and I'd always felt like a part of Paul's family. My best friend Vicki was even marrying his brother. No more Sunday dinners at Paul's mum's, no more big family parties and goodbye lovely apartment in St Heliers.

The business was going so well neither of us wanted to walk away from it, so we did the sensible thing and carried on as normal at work. The only change was that we stopped sharing an office. It was very odd saying goodnight to someone I'd been going home with for the last three years. I tried not to think about it by keeping myself so busy I didn't have time to think about it.

The apartment was sold and we split the money down the middle. With a small mortgage I was able to buy a little townhouse in Remuera. It had a gorgeous courtyard with a fountain and I'd sit out there for hours with the girls reading and learning scripts.

Because New Zealand's population was so small we needed a constant supply of new products to keep the wheel turning. In the States, one good product marketed well with a TV infomercial could keep a company like ours going for years and make an absolute fortune. Here I felt as if I was on a treadmill and couldn't get off – we simply had to keep finding new products, filming more ads and writing more advertorials. It was neverending.

I wrote and filmed several thirty-minute infomercials for weight-loss tapes, a stop-smoking course, the Natural Glow Beauty Club and my own range of skincare products called Perfect Skin. Just when I thought we couldn't get any busier, the whole exercise market went through the roof with a variety of equipment that would all fit under a bed. In quick succession, we had the Ab Rocker, the Ab Roller and the Ab Flex. They were followed by the Easy Rider, the Jane Fonda Stepper and the All In One Gym.

We had a twenty-four-hour call centre and we moved into bigger premises in Penrose. The warehouse was about the size of a football pitch. It was before the whole internet-shopping thing and if people didn't want to wait for their goods to be delivered they'd call in and ask at reception if they could purchase them there.

Denise, our receptionist at the time, was always happy to oblige, running to the warehouse to fetch whatever they wanted. She was a gung-ho saleswoman, full of life and energy, but she got so busy trotting back and forth with stock that she asked if we could put some display shelves up behind her.

As the company grew, more and more people kept arriving to buy the latest gadgets and, eventually, we employed someone else to help her out. Even so, the two women were so busy selling they didn't have time to do much day-to-day office work. We bought the building next door and turned it into a huge as-seen-on-TV shop. Later on, we opened another one in Wellington and one in Christchurch. Where would it all end?

Paul and I thought our business had grown quite steadily but to everyone else it seemed phenomenal. Within four years, we moved offices three times and ended up with about one hundred and twenty staff in Auckland and another one hundred and fifty in Australia. My ads were also screening in Hong Kong, Malaysia, Taiwan, Singapore, Russia, South Africa and Fiji!

I was also asked to do motivational speeches all over the country. The media's interest in me increased and I appeared on various programmes, such as *20/20* and *Made in New Zealand*. Every week I was in some newspaper or magazine and everyone was asking the same questions – 'How did you become so successful?' 'Why did you come to New Zealand?' 'Why did you decide to stay in Auckland?' They'd obviously never been to Wolverhampton!

Being the subject of so much publicity still seemed a bit strange and I couldn't understand all the fuss. I had a good laugh when I read that I was an overnight success – it had only taken me twenty years!

I started getting invited to appear on TV shows as a celebrity guest, and felt right at home – I loved performing and making people laugh. I was bored with selling things and felt like I needed a new challenge. I decided I would have my own TV show.

I really felt like I'd made it. I didn't have to worry about paying my bills, or what would happen if I got sick and had to take time off. I felt I was successful and would never have to struggle ever again. It was a wonderful feeling.

I loved going to the supermarket. For years, I used to wander down the aisles with a list and a calculator, making sure I kept to a strict budget. Now I could spend a couple of hours pushing my trolley around and buy whatever I fancied. Roast beef, smoked salmon and a few fancy cheeses – I'd end up with an overflowing trolley and enough food to feed the New Zealand army. It was all a bit daft because there was only me.

I didn't do any entertaining. I only had a couple of friends. Occasionally I'd go out with Susie, who used to work for me and lived just around the corner. I also went back to England once a year, mainly to look for new products at the Ideal Home Show. It was strange walking round seeing all my old friends still demonstrating the same old things. I was so glad it wasn't me. I'd make a flying visit to see family and friends, and to make sure Mum was okay. She had a live-in boyfriend, but he wasn't up to much and they were always falling out.

By now, my dad had moved to Lancashire to live with his

partner, Edna, and it was nice to see him happy at last.

During a stopover in Singapore, on the way back from one of my trips home, I was in my hotel room and turned the TV on for company. Unpacking my suitcase, I glanced over to the TV and there I was demonstrating the Suzanne clip. I was looking at myself on screen thinking, 'My God, I must be jet-lagged because I can't understand a word I'm saying apart from Suzanne clip'. Then the penny dropped – apart from those two words the commercial had been dubbed in Cantonese. I was beside myself with laughter as tears rolled down my face. It's still one of the funniest things I've ever seen!

All in all, life was wonderful. The only thing missing was someone to share it all with. I was lonely most of the time and wondered if I'd ever meet the right man or have children. It was something I'd been thinking about more and more, especially since Vicki had baby Jessica. It made me long for a child of my own, but at the age of thirty-eight I knew time was running out.

Prestige Marketing was going from strength to strength. I was still flying to Sydney to appear on the Bert Newton show to sell my wares and I was thrilled to get a call to say Julian Clary was appearing on the show and that he was a big fan of mine. He had asked if we could do something together!

Vicki came on the show with me, and the three of us laughed like little kids as I tried to show him how all my gadgets worked. I couldn't wait to tell everyone back in England that I'd worked with Julian Clary – they'd be so impressed.

Ever since I'd decided I should have my own TV show I'd been popping into Television New Zealand with one idea or another, which they'd very politely turn down. Every other month, I'd go to try and talk them into making my latest sure-fire hit show. But once again fate stepped in to lend me a helping hand. After a function one night I accidentally got into a taxi that had been ordered by another woman. We were going in the same direction so we decided to share the ride. When I found out I was in a taxi with the head of programming for TV3 I took the opportunity to tell her about my ideas. We arranged to meet for lunch and a couple of months later I was filming my *Style Challenge* show with Julie Christie's Touchdown Productions. It was one of the first reality shows made in New Zealand and it proved to be a winner. Each week I would go to someone's house and look through their wardrobe and drawers to see what they usually wore. Then we'd go shopping for a new outfit. The woman would then get a fabulous make-over and hairdo, before 'revealing' herself to her partner in a flash restaurant. I loved seeing the difference it made to these women to have a special day of being pampered and being made to feel attractive again. I cried every week.

There was yet another new boss at TVNZ so I went back with some more ideas and, four months later, had a contract to film two series of *Guess Who's Coming to Dinner*. It had taken me five years to sell the idea. Once again my persistence and perseverance had paid off.

While all this was going on, I was still writing and filming infomercials and Paul was negotiating with an American direct-marketing company called Quantum Global. They wanted to buy us out. It didn't seem real when, several months later, we all sat around a table and Paul and I signed away Prestige Marketing and Suzanne Paul Australia. Apparently we were to receive thirty-nine million dollars. The look on my face must have been priceless.

Never give in, never give in, never, never, never, never

That is a quote from one of Winston Churchill's most famous speeches, and I often think of it when I know that I need to be persistent and to persevere. Sometimes you just have to keep going.

Whenever I think 'What's the point?' it helps if I look back on my earlier life, to when things suddenly changed for the better. There have been numerous occasions when I've lost hope and struggled to stay strong. Then, unexpectedly, something wonderful has happened and, next minute, I'm on cloud nine. If it's happened to me before, it's happened to other people, too, and it can happen to me again. I just have to hang in there and believe everything will come out right.

The sun will come out tomorrow

I love that daft song from *Annie*. It always makes me feel good. It gives me hope that tomorrow could well be a better day than today and could turn out to be the best day of my life. One day it will be – I can guarantee it.

If you are losing, very soon you are going to win.

If I'm feeling really low, I always pop along to the library and take out a few inspirational biographies. I like reading about people who have succeeded against all odds. I tell myself that if they can do it, so can I!

Every day amazing things happen to people just like you and me.

Stick to your guns

If you think you have a good idea and you feel really passionate about it, give it everything you've got to make it a reality. It doesn't matter *what* I do – great or small – I throw myself into it one hundred per cent. I get so passionate about the things I want to do and the products I want to launch that people are often amazed at my energy and vitality. I get so excited about my latest plan that other people are drawn in and they begin to feel excited, too. It's the passion that creates the energy I need to keep going.

If people keep turning you down and think your ideas are wrong, just say to yourself, 'It's only one man's opinion today'.

A change is as good as a rest

Sometimes you have to leave your comfort zone and try something different. It may even be something that you fear doing.

I dreaded filming those first TV commercials – I was sick with worry. I wouldn't sleep the night before and I couldn't wait for it to be over. Later, filming became something I enjoyed doing more than anything else in the world. It still is.

Push yourself out of your comfort zone and to your limits. Remember, the brave do not live forever, but the cautious do not live at all.

Yes, you probably will be frightened but at least you'll know you're alive. You never know what you'll excel at, until you try. Every time I turn up for a speaking engagement I think to myself, 'Never again, what was I thinking? What if they don't like me? What if I forget what I'm saying? What if they don't get my jokes?' I say to Duncan, 'This is the last time I'm doing anything like this'. But the feeling you get when you've finished is addictive. I feel as if I could conquer the world. I'm absolutely euphoric because I was terrified, but I did it anyway. It's the best feeling in the world!

Over the years, I've tried my hand at various things that put the fear of God into me. I found I was really good at some of those things – at others I was useless. But I didn't care. I'd just try something else.

Since I've been in New Zealand, I've had ice-skating, tap and ballet lessons and I've had a go at hip-hop. I've learnt to speak French and taste wine. I've taken classes in singing, acting and belly dancing and studied art, scrap-booking, yoga, and Pilates.

Don't let fear hold you back.

The brave do not
live forever, but the
cautious do not live
at all.

Notes

9

I'll be glad when I've had enough!

Just before Paul and I sold the companies, I had a birthday and went with my friend Susie for a meal at Iguaçu. The restaurant was really popular at the time and afterwards we stayed to have a drink at the bar.

A young man, a friend of Graham's, started chatting me up. Graham was the guy I'd sold sunglasses at a pharmacy for, a few years before. We went out to dinner a couple of nights later and, although we weren't entirely compatible, his easy-going nature suited me at the time. Dean seemed to know everyone in town and we were always going to parties and dinners. It was nice to have someone to go to functions with. Up until then my life had always been work, work, work and more work.

I remember the first time he took me to Ashburton to meet his family. I had to go out and buy some casual clothes. All I had was rack after rack of business suits. There were dozens of them in every colour and style – every time I filmed a new ad, I bought a new suit.

When we finally sold the companies for thirty-nine million, most of that was in stocks and shares. I got a couple of million dollars in cash, which I expected would last me the rest of my life, anyway. I wasn't worried, especially as the shares were listed on the New York stock exchange at around twenty-two dollars. Everyone told me that shares were like money in the bank.

In England, I was featured on the six o'clock news – all my friends and family watched, with their mouths hanging open when they heard the story of the woman who had left Wolverhampton with five pounds and had now sold her company in New Zealand for thirty-nine million dollars! My phone nearly rang right off the wall in Remuera.

Both Paul and I were contracted to the company for five years but could sell our shares after one year. The cash I had only had to last a couple of years at the most, and then I could sell up.

I still had it in my mind that I wanted to live somewhere looking out to sea. Real estate agents were looking for the ideal house for me. To begin with there was nothing at the right price, but when I went to see a property on the cliff in Glendowie I completely fell in love with the view. A sense of peace washed over me as I stood there looking out to Browns Island, but the house was so run down and dilapidated it would have to be knocked down. Dean assured me it was cheaper to build your own home, anyway. He'd done that sort of thing before and he could be the project manager. I bought the land and got plans drawn up for the dream home that I'd seen in my mind for years.

The actor Michael Caine said it took him a long time before he could save any money because, first, he had to look after his family and friends. He was right. It is no good living in luxury, if people you know and love are living in poverty and squalor. As soon as I had some money I flew over to England to make sure everyone was okay. I gave money away like sweets and loved every minute. I was able to buy my friend Kathy a house so she and her family could move out of the rough council estate I'd stayed at, in another lifetime. Mum came back to New Zealand with me and I bought her a gorgeous apartment at Grace Joel Retirement Village. She absolutely loved it there and made lots of new friends. In fact, she went on to marry one of the other residents – a wonderful man called Harold.

My brother Bill got one of the brand new apartments on Princes Wharf and I bought another as an investment. Dean also signed us up for an apartment on the Gold Coast and an office block in the city and we even splashed out on a luxury yacht. Dean had dozens of friends and they all enjoyed our celebrity lifestyle.

About then, I received a phone call from England from a TV production company – Carlton. They wanted to make a documentary about me, to be shown on British television. It was part of a series they were doing about millionaires and they sent me an episode on Richard Branson so I could see the format.

I was thrilled to be taking part. Not only did they capture my lifestyle in New Zealand, I also flew back to Wolverhampton where they filmed me visiting my old haunts. It was a strange feeling going back to the street where I spent my childhood. Some of my old neighbours were still there, and we chatted about the good old days. Betty, who'd washed my hair for me all those years ago, was now an old lady and we shed a few tears together at our shared memories.

As I drove away everyone in the narrow street came out to watch the stretch limo trying to turn the corner. It took us about six attempts to get around and it must have looked very comical as we kept inching forward then back again, then forward. It wasn't quite the glamorous exit I'd dreamed about, but near enough.

Going back to my old school was the worst thing. I could see myself all those years ago – a sad, lonely child trying desperately to fit in. The same old feelings washed over me as I walked through the school gates. All the kids clamoured around the car, hoping to see a visiting pop star or somebody famous and were disappointed when they saw me. They were all shouting to one another, 'Who is it? Who's in the limo?' I could hear the replies, 'She's nobody. Just someone that went to our school.' She's nobody. All these years later and going to school felt the same.

They called the programme 'Glow Girl' and it went on to win a Bafta for documentary of the year. It was never shown in New Zealand.

I knew when Dean asked me to marry him that our relationship was far from perfect. But I thought at the age of forty the whole marriage and baby thing was nearly beyond my reach and it was probably the best offer I was going to get. I was frightened of being on my own again. Loneliness is the worst feeling in the world and I'd had enough of it in my life.

Like a lot of women, I was more swept away by the thought of the wedding than the actual marriage. I spent months planning the whole thing down to every tiny detail. I was going to have the perfect wedding – no expense spared!

We tied the knot on a lovely sunny day, in a beautiful Catholic church at the end of a little cul-de-sac. I'd flown in twenty-five of my friends and family from England for the trip of a lifetime. They stopped off for an all-expenses-paid holiday in Los Angeles and after the wedding they all went to Australia for another week there. The best thing about having money was seeing the pleasure it bought to other people. As well as flying in my Aunty Jean and her family from Sydney, I shouted them a trip to England – Jean hadn't been back for thirty years. I wanted to thank them for looking after me when I had nothing.

The whole wedding was like something out of Hollywood. I'd sold the rights to a women's magazine but I thought we'd kept the whole thing pretty hush-hush, until we pulled up to the church. The car was surrounded by dozens of photographers all pushing their cameras at the windows, flashes going off ten to the dozen. I stepped out of the Rolls-Royce and asked who was from the *Woman's Day*. One at a time they all put their hands up claiming to be from *Woman's Day*.

I had to laugh – it was like the scene out of the movie *Spartacus* when they all claim to be him! One of my best memories from that day is when my father walked me down the aisle. He's from that era when you didn't show your feelings and you certainly didn't talk about them. The music started and as we set off he said to me, 'You haven't done too bad, have you?' It was the nicest thing he'd ever said to me and I started bawling my eyes out. By the time I got to the altar I was a complete mess.

You can hear me on the wedding video saying, 'Emotions, get

back in your room. I'll deal with you later.' That's a tip I read in a book once, for when you need to pull yourself together. It aways works for me.

The reception was held in a marquee at Kelliher Estate, on beautiful Puketutu Island. It was outrageously expensive, but I wanted a day that we'd all remember, even if it was going to cost me well over one hundred thousand dollars!

The honeymoon was even more extravagant. We flew to London where we shopped up a storm, then on to Paris for more of the same – first class all the way. In Italy we visited Rome and Florence before catching up with friends in a village called Perugia, then made our way to Venice, all the time shopping and more shopping. We spent three days going through Europe on the Orient Express and arrived home three weeks later with eight suitcases of stuff and lots of photos. One of those suitcases was full of baby clothes.

As soon as we were married, we started trying for a baby. I'd heard a lot about IVF over the years – if you couldn't get pregnant naturally, you just went along for treatment and, next minute, you were pregnant. I'd read about celebrities who'd become pregnant the first time they tried IVF and it was becoming more common for women to have babies in their forties. I couldn't wait. I'd lived by the rule – Keep trying until you get what you want. This would be the same. I wanted to be pregnant and I thought it was inevitable that I would, one day soon, become pregnant.

I was shocked when the fertility specialist told me I only had about a fifteen per cent chance of ever becoming pregnant and the chances would decrease the older I got.

I wanted to believe I'd be one of the lucky ones so, like everything else I set my mind to, it was all I talked about. It was all I thought about. My whole future happiness depended on me getting pregnant. I became obsessed with having a baby and it nearly destroyed me.

I don't think any amount of reading could have prepared me for the pain and indignities you have to put your body through during IVF. I'd always had a terrible fear of needles and can remember screaming the place down, when I'd had injections as a kid. Now I had to inject myself twice a day in the stomach. It doesn't matter how many times you practice on an orange, it doesn't make it any easier when you have to push that needle into your own flesh. You also have to take tablets and visit the clinic very early in the morning for blood tests. All in all, the whole procedure completely takes over your life.

Everything revolves around the treatment. The combination of drugs sloshes about in your stomach all night, so you can't sleep. You feel sick all the time, so you can't eat. After a month of injecting yourself, it's time for an internal scan to see how many eggs you've managed to create. Then the eggs are measured every other day to see how they're growing.

Then there are the drugs to stop you ovulating, and the drugs to start you ovulating again.

Having the eggs removed is both incredibly painful and exciting all at the same time. You feel so full of hope that this is it – you're on the way to becoming a parent. Over the course of a week you can see the eggs growing and multiplying, getting stronger and, eventually, being fertilised. It's so incredible to witness this miniscule life-form changing so dramatically.

During this time, you take drugs to fool your body that

> I don't think any amount of reading could have prepared me for the pain and indignities you have to put your body through during IVF.

it's pregnant so that when the fertilised eggs are put back, it's the right environment for them to thrive. A week after the transplant, you have a blood test to find out whether or not you're pregnant.

It's a funny feeling, knowing that a simple phone call is going to completely change your life for ever. At the appointed time, I went to make the call and found my hands were shaking so much I couldn't dial the number. I could not believe it when I was told that I was not pregnant. Once the shock had worn off, the tears flowed. The cruellest side-effect of the drug that makes you feel pregnant is that you actually look pregnant. Your stomach swells up and everyone congratulates you and pats the bump. I was even shown in the newspaper once, with a story that I was pregnant. Everywhere I went I had to deny the story while my heart was breaking.

It's like having a miscarriage. You think you're pregnant. Your body has tricked you into believing you're pregnant, and the next minute you're not. The dream has been shattered. You grieve for the little baby you thought was growing inside you.

During all of the procedures I couldn't be far from the fertility clinic and it began to get really difficult to carry on filming my TV shows. After the hit series *Guess Who's Coming to Dinner* I filmed a series of *Garage Sale* and then *Second Honeymoon*, as well as writing and filming new ads.

Building had started and the new house was underway, complete with a nursery. By the fifth IVF attempt, going out, especially to family events, had become an absolute nightmare for me. Dean had three brothers and it seemed as if someone was always pregnant or about to give birth, or had just had a baby. I wanted to scream and cry and say it was unfair. Why not me? Instead, I used my performance face to ooh and aah over the bundles of joy and waited until I got home to break down.

All our friends had children and I couldn't join in any conversations about parenting. I felt like an outsider and a failure. I'd stand with the men round the barbecue, so I wouldn't have to listen to the latest childbirth story. I would have given anything to be able to join in.

In the end I just stopped going out – it was less painful. I stopped reading women's magazines – every week they extolled the joys of motherhood. According to them, I would never know what real love was, unless I gave birth. I could never be really happy until I had a child to care for and my life would have no meaning until I had created a life.

As well as IVF, I also tried every alternative method that I could find. Twice a day I swallowed sixteen tablets and drank disgusting black liquid from a naturopath. I had acupuncture and crystals waved over me. I didn't drink or smoke for five years, and I only ate organic food. If someone had told me to put teabags on my head and run naked over the hills, I'd have done that as well.

By now, Dean and I were arguing about everything from the door knobs to the bath taps for the new house and by the time I had my eighth course of IVF we were leading completely separate lives. We only saw each other in the morning at 6 am before Dean left for the gym and when he came home again at about 10 pm. For the last two years of our marriage I felt more alone than ever before.

On top of all the IVF drama, since Paul and I had sold the company it had gone from bad to worse. I'd only managed to sell a few of my shares before the price hit an all-time low of one dollar – they were practically worthless.

Being on TV shows in New Zealand doesn't pay much and my money had slowly dwindled away, especially after several bad investments that included a fishing boat, a housing company, power drinks, steel-backed bricks and Dean's latest venture – mobile-phone domain names.

Even getting a cute new puppy didn't make me smile. I was weary and tired of life. I couldn't see an end to the misery. I asked Dean to take the dog back to the breeder; I couldn't cope with it and I thought it deserved to be with someone who could love it properly. Luckily, the puppy stayed.

It seemed on the outside that I had it all, but on the inside I was falling apart. I was a physical and mental wreck. I went about day-to-day tasks but found no joy in anything. I was crying constantly. I fell off the edge and went into a depression that I was scared I'd never come out of.

Enough is enough

The hardest part for me during this time was working out when to give up. I'd spent my life believing that if I kept on trying and gave it another go, I'd be successful.

When do you stop? When do you say, 'I've tried my best but it's not meant to be'?

When do you give up on a baby? A marriage? A dream?

It would have been a relief if someone had said, 'You can stop now. It's not going to work for you.'

I went to see clairvoyants, mediums and psychics. I rang the horoscope hotlines hoping they'd say, 'You're wasting your time. It's never going to work for you.' I wanted someone to help me make the decision.

In the end, it became obvious to me that I couldn't keep going – because it was impossible to carry on. You just know, sometimes, that you can't keep going.

CLOSED FOR REPAIRS
Nervous breakdown, depression, a trip to La-La Land – whatever you call it, sometimes your brain switches into repair mode and you can't function properly. It's scary because you have no idea how long this state is going to continue, and it doesn't matter what you do, the only thing you feel is sad.

I didn't go for counselling. I didn't need to talk about it. I'd already spent years talking about nothing else. I didn't want to talk about it anymore – it was too painful.

I realised that before I could feel better and be happy again, I had to grieve for the life I'd lost. I'd made endless plans and had dozens of dreams about my new life as a mother. There were so many milestones I would never experience and so many memories I would never have. There was so much joy beyond my reach. I cried every day and I'm crying now, as I feel the desperation all over again.

One day at a time

When you're healing, you have to look after yourself and protect yourself.

I didn't read newspapers or magazines – they might have stories that would upset me. I never watched the news on TV or listened to it on the radio. I didn't put myself in a situation that would set me off. It was better to say no to an invitation to a christening than spend four days crying about it. I wouldn't listen to soulful, dreary music. I wouldn't sit about wallowing in self-pity for hours. I took St John's wort and tried to carry on with a normal life. I prayed that one day I wouldn't feel as bad. And one day, I didn't.

The hardest part is trying not to feel bitter and resentful when you see other people having what you want but will never be able to have.

You have to learn to let it go.

You have to find happiness somewhere else.

I prayed that
one day I wouldn't
feel as bad.
And one day,
I didn't.

Notes

10

What were you thinking?

While all the IVF drama was going on, Mum was taken ill with liver problems and spent weeks in hospital, followed by several months recuperating in a nursing home. At the same time, her husband Harold – who had Parkinson's disease – deteriorated rapidly, and followed the same route. He went into hospital and then into a nursing home, but he never came out.

As Mum got better, I took her to visit Harold every day. We'd put my cocker spaniel puppy, Walnut the Wonder Dog, up on the bed. Harold loved to pet her and Walnut, seeming to sense that Harold was poorly, just lay still beside him.

When Harold died, Mum didn't want to live at the retirement village any more, so I rented her a lovely apartment on The Parade in St Heliers. Dean and I were living in a townhouse there while our mansion was being built.

Every night Mum would cook dinner for me, and Walnut and I would walk up the road to eat and spend the night watching TV with her. Dean and I didn't eat a meal together for about two years. Having Mum close by helped me keep going through some dark days.

Things improved again for us when my brother Phillip immigrated to New Zealand with his wife and three teenage boys. I rented a house for them a stone's throw away and stopped by every day for a cuppa and a chat. For the first time in years, I had all the family apart from Dad together and we had some good, fun times. I was nearly back to my old self. But my marriage never recovered and even after Dean and I moved into the big house we continued to lead separate lives.

Just before Christmas 2001 we had a spectacular fancy-dress house-warming party for about a hundred people. I flew my dad and Edna and my Uncle Ken over and they stayed in the guest quarters we'd had built on the grounds. Because it was such a long driveway we had golf buggies ferrying people from the gate, and guests were greeted by Santa and his naughty elf – a very rude dwarf – who hurled abuse at people all night.

The house had three levels. The top storey had three bedrooms with ensuite bathrooms. The ground floor had the living quarters, with two lounges and a kitchen looking out to sea. The basement was the entertaining floor. There was a home theatre, gym and sun-bed room as well as a full-sized pool table, lounge and hotel-sized bar area that opened to a swimming pool and a garden, which led down to the beach. It was one of my childhood dreams to have seven toilets – one for every day of the week!

It was the perfect house for parties and I loved living there, but it soon became obvious that with a bundle of worthless shares and none of our more recent investments making money, we couldn't afford the upkeep.

It was time to make some new plans and make some drastic changes in my life. Walnut the Wonder Dog had melted my heart with her funny little ways, and I couldn't imagine how I'd once asked Dean to take her back to the kennels. In the end, I kept the dog and got rid of the husband.

There was no big drama. One Saturday night I did the 'I think we need to talk' speech and Dean moved into our city apartment the next day. I'd seen it coming for months, but it was still a shock to realise my marriage was over after only five years.

It was an even bigger shock when I discovered the state of our finances. I needed to start earning some serious money – not the peanuts TV work paid.

I also had no choice but to put the mansion up for sale as quickly as possible. I was advised to put it out to tender but, after several months of expensive advertising, the tender date came and went and the house hadn't sold. It was hard to put a value on the property. It really depended on what someone was prepared to pay for the privacy and spectacular views. It had become a sought-after area to live in and one of New Zealand's richest men, Graeme Hart, lived just up the road.

On a good day, the house could have fetched anywhere between five and six million dollars and I'd have been away laughing. But it didn't. No one could tell me why. Maybe people didn't want all their money tied up in one massive house. Anyway, things were getting desperate, and I felt lonely rattling round in that huge house by myself. I didn't want to be on my own, but I dreaded having to do that whole dating thing again. I wasn't really one for standing around in a bar drinking.

Being married to Dean for five years hadn't put me off men and I certainly wasn't going to hold all men responsible for his behaviour. On the contrary, I used the experience to pinpoint exactly what qualities I required in a partner, which was easy to do now that I knew exactly what I didn't want!

I always thought that somebody up there knew what they were doing. I never doubted that I would meet my Mr Right. I had no idea where or when, but I had the feeling that if I was looking for him, then he would be out there somewhere looking for me. When the time was right, we'd find each other. And we did.

Once again it was my friend Susie who talked me into going out with her. We went to Soul, a popular bar on Auckland Harbour's viaduct basin. It was not too busy on a Saturday night and we sat at a table near the bar. A succession of men ambled over for a chat throughout the night. One of them was a tall, good-looking, young man who introduced himself as Duncan. Not only was he charming, but he was funny, too.

I wasn't sure if Susie had her eye on him and she'd been single for a while so I thought I should see how the land lay. I pointed out that Duncan had a lovely smile and beautiful eyes and, although she agreed, she said he wasn't her type. I didn't think he was my type either. He was younger than me and that had been one of the problems with Dean. The seven-year age difference meant he wanted to be out every night partying while I wanted to stay at home with a good book.

Plus, I imagined someone as gorgeous as Duncan would have his pick of the ladies and I didn't want to go through the drama of being dumped for a younger, prettier model.

I'd thought my ideal man would have all of Duncan's attributes, but be a successful businessman aged about 55. I played the game anyway, because I felt a connection between us and I hadn't enjoyed myself nearly so much for a long time. It felt good to feel attractive and gave my confidence a much-needed boost. Still, when he asked me out to dinner I panicked. 'No thanks,' I said, and picked up my handbag and hurried out the door.

Over the next couple of months I went with Susie to Soul every week, but Duncan was nowhere to be seen. I started to wish I'd taken him up on his offer. My self-esteem was really low and at forty-six I felt like the oldest swinger in town.

Then, one night, there he was and my heart leapt into my mouth at the sight of him. Feeling like a brazen hussy, I went straight up to him and asked if he'd like a drink. He said, 'Yes please, and I'd still like to take you out to dinner.' This time I accepted. His beautiful face lit up and I nearly melted right then and there.

He called the next day, and I invited him to escort me to the première of the Austin Powers film *Goldmember* at Skycity Theatre. I thought it was best to get it over with, so I warned him there'd be lots of celebrities and photographers there. He didn't seem fazed. If he couldn't cope with the attention, we could call it quits before things went any further – it would save a lot of heartache later on. Our photograph was in every newspaper and magazine across the country afterwards and, although we had both had a fabulous night, Duncan looked a lot like a deer in the headlights.

Around that time I was appearing in the TV show *How's Life?*. It was an agony-aunt show that screened every week night at 5.30 pm and Duncan was working as a chef in the city. We saw each other twice a week, spoke on the phone four times a day

> *As soon as I set foot inside the Fishermans Wharf building, although it had been empty for a few years, I knew that was it.*

and sent each other about thirty-five texts a day! We were like a couple of love-struck teenagers and we did much of our courting by text message. Despite the ten-year age gap, I'd fallen head over heels in love and within four months Duncan had moved in with me. I couldn't remember ever feeling so happy. The only spanner in the works was money – or the lack of it. The house still hadn't sold, and the only way I could earn enough to continue living there was to start some sort of business with what little cash I had left.

The idea for Rawaka surfaced as we were driving to Napier to visit Duncan's kids. It was something I'd been thinking about for years and with Duncan being a chef I thought it was something we could do together.

At Prestige Marketing, we had hosted a lot of overseas businesspeople and it was up to me to show them around and try to give them a feel for New Zealand's culture. I also used to get a steady stream of visitors from England and I wanted them to see why I loved the country so much. Often, time was limited and people couldn't get down to Rotorua – they never got to see a cultural performance or taste a delicious hangi.

I felt sure that, one day, somebody would realise the huge potential of an Auckland-based venture that would make it possible for visitors to get a uniquely New Zealand cultural experience without leaving the city. One day that somebody was me.

Duncan and I looked at several venues but as soon as I set foot inside the Fishermans Wharf building, although it had

LEFT: Mum's wedding to Harold. I'm with my brother Billy. My friend's daughter, Jessica, is the flowergirl.

BELOW: Me and my dad at my first wedding.

ABOVE LEFT: My first wedding to Dean.

ABOVE RIGHT: Me on my honeymoon on the *QEII*.

BELOW: Baby in a box – she loved boxes.

ABOVE: This is Walnut the Wonder Dog with a bad hair day.

BELOW LEFT: Walnut the Wonder Dog at four weeks old.

BELOW RIGHT: Me and Lily in 1994. She's sixteen now.

ABOVE: Me on our cruiser *Galileo*.

BELOW: The Big House lit up for Christmas.

ABOVE: Me in the pool at the Big House.

BELOW: Me on the balcony of the Big House.

ABOVE: Me and Mum with my hero Gene Pitney.

BELOW: Me and Mum with John Rowles, who uses Natural Glow.

ABOVE: The best day of my life, July 2005.

LEFT: Me and my soul mate, Duncan.

ABOVE LEFT: Me in costume for *Dancing with the Stars*. (EMMA BASS/ NEW ZEALAND WOMAN'S WEEKLY)

ABOVE: Me and Stefano in rehearsa mode. (FRANCES OLIVER/NEW ZEALAND WOMAN'S WEEKLY)

LEFT: Hard at work during rehearsa (FRANCES OLIVER/NEW ZEALAND WOMAN' WEEKLY)

been empty for a few years, I knew that was it. The location was perfect – just a short ride over the Harbour Bridge from the city centre with fantastic views back to the city. It needed a lot of work to make it viable, but we did the numbers and negotiated a long lease.

A friend recommended someone to be our cultural liaison officer to assist us with protocol and who would be able to apply for funding from various Government agencies. We also employed a great guy who specialised in tourism and event management because we needed to start taking bookings straightaway, ready for when we planned to opened the following summer.

Just before renovations started, I was asked to take part in *Celebrity Treasure Island* and even though reality shows didn't pay much, it was an opportunity to remind the bosses at TVNZ that I was still around. I'd been trying for the last couple of years to persuade them to let me have a new TV show. They did revive *Guess Who's Coming to Dinner* for a season, but put Mike King and Stacey Daniels in as co-presenters. I loved entertaining people and making them laugh, so *Treasure Island* was a great opportunity, plus I got to spend a couple of weeks on a beautiful Fijian island.

Mum was living with us at the time but Duncan was able to keep an eye on her for me. I did wish I was twenty years younger when I saw Nicky Watson, Greer Robson and Eva the Bulgarian in their bikinis, but I didn't look too bad for my age. The hardest part for me was the lack of sleep. Even at home in my warm comfy bed, I'd toss and turn and get up two or three times each night. On the island, I lay awake for hours on the hard sand with crabs running over me, squashed up against six other women. Even the sleeping pills I'd smuggled in had no effect.

It was the women versus the men and our camps were right

next door to each other. We were forbidden to fraternise with the enemy but at 6 pm each day when the film crew left the island for the night, we would all sit together around a camp fire and cook up any food we'd won during the day. There was never enough food and we were always hungry, especially the men. What little food we had was always full of sand and tasted of smoke. I lost nearly five kilograms during the ten days I was there.

The toilet facilities were a big problem, especially for the women. Basically, there weren't any. We had to walk into the trees, dig a hole and do our ablutions as best we could, except I couldn't. With everyone wandering about the island looking for fruit or firewood, I'd hear a rustle in the bushes and get stage fright. The other women were the same, and the most commonly asked question was, 'Have you been yet?'

After several sleepless nights, I was tired all the time. I found it hard to concentrate on the challenges that were set for us during the day and I started to feel quite dizzy and spaced out. I was just about over the whole experience when, in the middle of the night, a cyclone hit the island. The men's camp had blown down and they came running over to ours. We spent the rest of the night huddled together under a tarpaulin while the storm raged all around us.

Jason Gunn and I tried to keep everyone's spirits up by singing and acting daft. Even though we were all frozen and soaked to the skin, we had to laugh at Jason. He's a natural comedian who had us all in stitches. The last few hours before dawn I found myself spooning between him and Matthew Ridge as we tried to get warm and catch a couple hours sleep.

The crew arrived to rescue us early the next morning. We must have looked a right sorry bunch – everything we had was wet through.

All the girls were highly emotional and kept crying all the time. I was missing Duncan and desperately wanted to go home. The ban on mobile phones meant I hadn't spoken to him since my arrival on the island. After we'd all dried off we were taken back to carry on filming the show. I begged the others to vote me off at the next elimination – I was exhausted and worried about everything at home.

I'd only been back a few hours when Duncan proposed to me while we were making a cup of tea! We had an engagement party that night at home. It was also Duncan's thirty-seventh birthday and, although we didn't know it at the time, would be the best day we would have together in a long while.

I knew I had to
change the way
I thought about things
if I wanted to feel
better.

Change the way you think

It's not your circumstances that affect you. It's how you think about your circumstances that affects how you feel about them.

It had taken me several months to come out of the black hole I fell into after all the IVF treatments had failed, Dean and I had split up and I had to sell my dream home. I knew I didn't want to go back there.

The way I was thinking about things made me feel sad and unhappy. I knew I had to change the way I thought about things if I wanted to feel better.

Always look on the bright side of life

Different people react differently to the same circumstances.

I'm lucky that, by nature, I am a born optimist. I can usually see the positives in a situation but, sometimes, when my head's all over the place, I need to make myself do it.

I take the time to sit and think about things. For example, after my marriage broke up I would think about how wonderful it would be when my Mr Right found me. I thought about how kind and thoughtful he would be, how sexy and funny and genuine. I didn't miss Dean because I chose to focus on how wonderful my new partner was going to be. I thought about the two of us cosy and secure in the new townhouse I would buy. It was better than thinking about the multi-million-dollar mansion I couldn't afford to keep and a failed marriage.

Have a word with yourself

When you find your mind wandering and thinking about stuff that makes you feel sad, lonely, miserable, fed up, angry, resentful or just sorry for yourself, I've found the best thing I can do is tell myself to stop it! You can say it to yourself in your mind or out loud – it's up to you. But say it loud and clear.

Immediately think of something positive – anything positive. For example, it could be that your kids are all healthy or that you have a loving family around you, a lovely home or even that the dog's tail is wagging because he's pleased to see you. Then get active and *do* something.

If you have time to sit about thinking negative stuff that makes you feel bad, then you have time to do something that makes you feel good. You could read, write a letter to a faraway friend, phone someone you've been meaning to talk to for a while, or restart an old hobby. Go for a walk, make some new plans, anything.

One of the reasons I've taken up so many hobbies and classes over the years is so I haven't had time to think crap.

Make your mind up

You can't change how people behave, but you can change how you react to their behaviour.

Don't hold onto bitterness or resentment – you have to let it go or you're only causing yourself more pain. You have to believe that whoever caused you so much grief will get what they deserve in the end.

For your thinking to change your life, you have to believe what you're thinking. A lot of books advocate you say positive things in the present tense. For example:

- I have enough money to buy anything I want.
- I have my ideal partner.
- I live in a beautiful home.

It doesn't work for me. If I say these things and don't believe they are true, they don't make me feel good. I find it works better when I say things like:

- Money is on its way to me; I'll be able to buy anything I want.
- I know I'll meet my ideal partner, when the time is right.
- I'm looking forward to moving into my beautiful new home.

Remember, if you think differently, you'll act differently and if you act differently, you'll get different results.

Notes

11

Count your blessings

A week after our engagement, Duncan had to call for an ambulance to take me to hospital. The doctor suspected I had meningitis.

I didn't know what to say to Mum as I left for the hospital, she looked so frightened and I was, too. The pain in my head had become unbearable, I had a stiff neck and was vomiting and I knew that if it was bacterial meningitis I could die. Several hours later, as the many test results were returned, it was clear that I was, in fact, very lucky. I had viral meningitis.

Even though the hospital bed was tiny, Duncan insisted on lying beside me, right through the night. Whenever the nurse came in, she would tell him to get off. He did, but he'd get back on again as soon as she had left the room. I felt as if I could cope with anything as long as he was beside me.

After a couple of days, I was allowed home but was ordered to rest.

Slowly, as I regained my health, we continued to develop Rawaka. Just a few months into the development we started running into difficulties. Our cultural officer left unexpectedly and Duncan tried to track down the $300,000 worth of funding he told us he'd arranged. We couldn't find any paperwork, even though he'd assured us we were about to receive the money.

It took dozens of phone calls to discover that he hadn't applied for any funding from anywhere. We had to find some money fast.

Neither of us had ever raised funds at that level before and after ringing around several rich acquaintances, we had only managed to raise a third of the amount. It became obvious we needed a specialist to help us. We had people all over town trying to find us a business partner and I was selling off everything I owned to keep the workmen on the job. We knew we had to keep going because we were getting phone calls and enquiries from all over the world. We had to be ready by December, when the cruise ships would start arriving for the season.

We had rehearsals being held on the half-finished stage and costumes being made for the troupe. Duncan was building an amazing indoor replica Maori village and I was looking for Kiwi goods for the souvenir shop. We could see that we could go over budget as one thing after another had gone wrong – the wiring was shot, we needed a new floor in the kitchen and part of the roof had fallen in. And work had to be delayed for a while until we found an investor. There was more bad news to come. We were told we'd have to put in a lift – more money, more delays.

> It broke my heart to see thousands of tourists pouring into Auckland looking for things to do on rainy summer days.

This meant we weren't ready to open for the summer season. It broke my heart to see thousands of tourists pouring into Auckland looking for things to do on rainy summer days. When we were ready to open Auckland City was like a ghost town. We thought about laying all the staff off and closing for the winter, but we still had rent, rates and a mountain of outstanding bills to settle. Plus, everyone had worked so hard and the place looked so amazing that we decided to soldier on.

After a guided tour through the indoor replica village, visitors were seated in a round theatre restaurant where they were served a delicious traditional hangi with, of course, pavlova for dessert. After dinner there was a spectacular Polynesian show, an extravaganza of dance and music with fabulous costumes and lighting all put together by the irrepressible Mika. The first night, Duncan and I sat there and watched the show with tears running down our faces. It was awesome and people had travelled from all over the country to come and see it. I'm more proud of Rawaka than anything else I've achieved in my life. We made it happen and it was fabulous.

Weekends were busy, but mid-week there just weren't enough people around to make it worth opening. All my money had long gone to keep paying the staff. Even the house had been re-mortgaged.

We managed to stay open for three months, and then the newspapers ran a story under the headline: 'Padlocks go on the doors at Rawaka'. Our creditors were unsettled. No matter that the padlocks were always on the doors – it was the only way to lock them! The creditors thought it meant we'd been forced to close and started to demand payment. We had an emergency meeting with the liquidators but there was nothing we could do and Rawaka closed its doors for the last time in July 2004.

At the age of forty-eight, I had found true love but lost everything else. We lost our home and business. Duncan and I were completely broke.

I think the worst part of losing everything is the fear that's with you all the time. I was frightened to pick up the phone, afraid to answer the door, too scared to open the mail.

Every day people were looking for money or answers and I didn't have either. In the end, you go into shock as everything around you falls apart. You try to function as normal, while dealing with accountants, lawyers, liquidators and creditors. I tried to stay calm and do what was asked of me, but there were endless reports and documents and meetings to attend. I was smiling on the outside but going mad on the inside.

Some days I wanted to scream and one day I actually did. The banks forced the house sale to recover overdue mortgages and there was no money left to pay our other debts or to live on. When we received that phone call, it wasn't so much a scream as a wail. I knew the noise was coming from me, but I had no control over it. I didn't have control over anything anymore.

Two days later I stood in the St Heliers Bay dairy, crying. I didn't have enough money to pay for a few groceries and had to put them back on the shelves. I felt as if all eyes were on me and that I would die of shame.

We were broke and Duncan, Mum and I were about to become homeless. When a marketing company whose product I endorsed asked me to promote their makeup in pharmacies and shopping malls I saw this as a way of earning money to pay off my debts. I knew if I really got behind their product I could get the stores to stock it. I even flew over to Sydney several times for the company as well as promoting their product on TV and demonstrating it in malls. To be honest I couldn't think of anything worse than standing in a shop for six hours a day, saying the same things over and over. But I made myself look at the bigger picture and think about the end result. Still, it took every ounce of strength I had to keep doing it.

While things were pretty bad for us, at least Duncan and I had got through it together. So many people had said that he was only with me for my money. They had been proved wrong.

Sometimes, you meet really kind, genuine people. Thank God they seem to come along just when you need them most. During one of the many meetings with our lawyer, Ed, he told us he and his brothers had a rental property in Epsom that was empty. He said we could move in there as we didn't have anywhere else to go. We gratefully accepted his offer, promising to start paying rent as soon as we could afford to do so.

Six months after Rawaka closed its doors for the last time, I got a phone call that was, for me, as good as winning lotto. I was back on top of the world. TVNZ asked me to be in their new TV show called *Dancing with the Stars*. I was absolutely ecstatic. I'd been following the show in England and I knew it would be perfect for me – the dresses, the glitz and glamour, plus the chance to learn how to dance with a professional – it all sounded wonderful to me.

Life had become mundane and stressful, standing outside pharmacies saying the same thing over and over, always scrimping

> I was still crying when Paul Holmes asked me what I was going to do now I was bankrupt.

and scraping trying to pay the bills. The thought of being on *Dancing with the Stars* was just what we all needed – the show would give us something to talk about, apart from problems. Hopefully, it would also raise my profile again, so I could get more of the kind of work I loved – performing and entertaining people. Things were looking up at last and I had something wonderful to look forward to. I couldn't wait for the show to start. I just knew it would change my life.

Two months later a second phone call knocked me for six when someone from the show rang to say that the New Zealand production planned to stick to the British format and have a politician, an actress, a sportswoman and a bit of eye candy. It was pointed out to me that I was none of those things.

I was driving when I took the call and had to pull over. I couldn't see through the tears, and nothing I could say would make a difference. I wasn't in the show and that was that. Mum was upset when I told her, we'd all been looking forward to it so much it's all we'd talked about for weeks. I couldn't bear to see the disappointment on her face. I felt that I didn't want to risk getting excited about anything anymore, in case it didn't work out.

Things couldn't get any worse, except of course they did. The thing that I feared most would happen to me did.

I was standing in a shopping mall in Christchurch dusting powder on anyone who would keep still long enough. When I had a moment between customers, I switched my mobile on and saw I had several messages. Before I could check any of them, the phone rang. It was my agent, Karen Kay. She told me it had been reported in the news media that I'd been declared bankrupt. Everyone had been trying to get hold of me.

I went onto automatic pilot. Karen had already spoken to Duncan and they had arranged for me to appear on the *Holmes* show that night at 7 pm. Karen told me to go straight to the airport. A ticket had been booked for a flight to Auckland and a helicopter was on stand-by to fly me to the TV studio. It all felt surreal and I couldn't believe it was happening to me.

Duncan was waiting for me when I arrived. We just held onto each other and cried. Neither of us could speak. Someone put a microphone on me and I was hurried into the studio. I was still crying when Paul Holmes asked me what I was going to do now I was bankrupt.

It broke my heart to know that Mum was at home watching this on the television. I told Paul Holmes it didn't matter. Call it what you like, nothing had changed for me. I still felt the same as I had done that morning when I went to work in the mall. I already had my plan in action – I was helping to build another successful marketing company. I had new innovative products ready to be launched and as soon as the company was making a good profit I would pay the creditors. As soon as I earned the money, they could have it.

It sounded ridiculous to me that there was now a piece of paper saying I didn't have to pay them. Why was that? I'd already said I would pay my debts. It didn't make sense. I knew full well I owed that money and I knew I had to do whatever I could to pay it back. You don't need a lawyer to tell you the right thing to do – you know it in your heart.

Every night I stayed up later and later, exhausted but never wanting to go to sleep, because when I woke it would be morning and I'd have to face more problems, more fear, more panic. I was terrified that I was going to fall off the edge and that even Duncan wouldn't be able to catch me. I could barely function. I couldn't eat, I couldn't stop crying, I couldn't stop the madness in my head.

Mornings were the worst. I never thought I'd be able to get through the new day. I felt an overwhelming sadness and despair as I got ready to go and demonstrate make-up – again. I didn't want to be nice to people all day, I didn't have the energy. I wanted someone to save me. I wanted someone to say, 'Don't worry about it, go back to bed and it'll all go away.' But no one did.

The stress and worry was there all the time, like a heavy weight on my chest. I told Duncan to go. I felt it shouldn't be his problem. It wasn't what he thought he was getting into. I didn't expect him to stand by me, I thought it was too much to ask and I wouldn't ask it of him. God only knows what I would have done if he'd taken me at my word.

Being bankrupt isn't something you can forget about. Just as you think you feel a bit stronger and a wee bit hopeful, something happens that knocks the life right out of you again. One day, a girl from Vodafone rang to tell me they were closing my account – I couldn't have a mobile phone anymore. I didn't owe them any money, but it was company policy – they didn't deal with bankrupts. I felt humiliated and angry that some bit of a girl was treating me like a criminal. I don't know if I cried out of shame or anger. Both, I think.

You don't just lose your home, money and possessions when you're made bankrupt. You also lose your self-respect, confidence and dignity. There's not much left after that.

The bank closed my accounts and cancelled my credit cards. The only bank that would take me on was Kiwibank. Two gentlemen from the Official Assignee's Office walked around my home with a clipboard. Anything of value that was moveable was listed to see if it could be sold to raise money for creditors.

Mum was still living with us. She was frail and sad and I couldn't bear to see her looking that way. The guilt of letting everyone down and causing her so much pain was unbearable.

Around this time, the newspapers were full of stories about a little baby who had to have her limbs amputated after contracting bacterial meningitis. My heart went out to her and her family and their problems made mine seem insignificant. Everyone kept telling me I'd lost everything – it took the baby to make me realise it wasn't what I'd lost that mattered, but what I still had. So I put on my 'fake it till you make it' face and went out and smiled when I felt like screaming.

Every day above ground is a good day

Whenever you meet people that have recovered from a life-threatening illness, you notice how happy and content they are. They say things like, 'It was a terrible experience, but I'm a changed person because of it. I was so angry and unhappy before, now I'm just so happy to be alive.' The extreme situation, where they thought they might die, taught them to appreciate how wonderful their life really is.

When I contracted meningitis I became aware how lucky I was to be fit, strong and healthy. I realised all the things I'd been worrying about were quite trivial in comparison.

> **Don't wait until you lose something**
> **before you give it value.**
> **I was lucky, and so are you, if you have:**
> **Two of everything down the sides**
> **and one of everything down the middle.**
> **Then you should count your blessings.**

Every morning when I take Walnut for a walk, I thank God and the universe for all sorts of wonderful things – you can thank whoever you want.

Instead of focusing on all the things you don't have, take some time every day to be grateful for all the good things in your life. It might be the love of your partner, the health of your children, family and friends, a successful business, a lovely home or that you have recovered from an illness.

Everything you take for granted now, be thankful for, instead.

Good vibrations

There are dozens of books out there that explain the Law of Attraction. But, in a nutshell, whatever you focus on, you will attract more of the same – whether that's something negative or positive.

When Rawaka closed down all I thought about was going bankrupt. Every day I said to Duncan, 'I don't want to go bankrupt. Please don't let me go bankrupt.' In the end, the thing I gave most of my energy to thinking about became a reality.

So if you walk about all day moaning about how bad things are and how you have no money, you'll just attract more of the same.

Whereas, if you start the day saying, 'I'm so lucky to have my wonderful husband, and so happy that my family are close by, and I'm so glad the sun's shining and I have a good job', then you'll attract more wonderful things to you.

All I know is that by the time I get home from walking the dog I feel good about my life. I feel positive and happy.

COUNT YOUR BLESSINGS

Notes

12

Be more afraid of regret than failure

I knew in order to move forward I couldn't afford to give my time and energy to the bankruptcy. I couldn't keep thinking about it and talking about it. I had to focus on making some money to repay my debts. Duncan and I agreed that he would deal with anything relating to the bankruptcy — there was a mountain of paperwork, emails and meetings to get through. I would concentrate on new products, ad campaigns and demonstrating new products in the malls. Trying to get through the day without losing the plot was challenge enough.

It was bad enough being bankrupt, but to have the whole episode playing out under the media spotlight for all the world to witness was soul destroying.

I had to try and move on, but every time I went into the study the whole palaver was displayed in front of me. I found it hard to stay strong. So, I removed any visible signs of Rawaka, creditors and bankruptcy from my view – whether it was paperwork, computer files or letters. If I didn't see them, I didn't think about them – it was a bit like Scarlett O'Hara.

When everything went pear shaped, I thought about all the other times I'd hit rock bottom and had to start again with nothing. I realised if I followed the same steps as I had before I'd be able to pick myself up, even if I didn't feel like it. Then the idea came to me, to write all the steps down in a book so that other people could follow them. I rang Penguin to ask if they'd be interested in publishing it. I started thinking about the past and making notes about how I'd felt, how I'd looked at situations and what actions I'd taken. I knew that if I behaved the same way, I'd get the same results.

To get through those dark days we all needed something to look forward to, especially Mum, who was in constant pain from osteoporosis. On top of everything, she'd caught a very bad case of flu and all the coughing had broken several ribs. She seemed to be going downhill rapidly. She was on a waiting list to have a growth removed from her bladder, which turned out to be cancer.

I'd taken Mum to Fiji a couple of times and the warm climate and dry heat had taken her pain away – pain that even morphine had been unable to shift. Now, of course we didn't have money to pay for a holiday.

I put my thinking cap on and decided to see if one of the women's magazines would buy our wedding story. We could use the money to pay for the wedding and we could get married in Fiji!

In the end, the *New Zealand Woman's Weekly* decided to do the story and we set a date for 9 July 2005. I don't know who was more excited – Duncan, Mum or me. It seemed to give us all a new lease on life. We all had something to be happy about and positive to plan for after all the heartache of the previous year.

I'd already done the big white wedding with the sticky-out frock and this time I wanted something a lot simpler. The day wasn't going to be about matching the invitations to the menus and fancy flowers. It was about Duncan and me exchanging vows in front of our dearest friends and family. In the end, about twenty-five people joined us to celebrate and it was, without a doubt, the very best day of my whole life. I wore a beautiful pale pink gown encrusted with crystals and beads and I did my own hair and make-up. I don't think I've seen Duncan look more handsome in his Indian-style outfit, and my friend Vicki's two daughters made gorgeous bridesmaids.

I missed having my dad there to share my special day. This time I couldn't afford to fly him over, but both my brothers were there and I thought Mum would explode with happiness. All our troubles seemed so far away.

The day after the wedding we had a bit of drama when we found out one of our guests had organised to sell photos to a rival magazine. If our wedding photographs appeared in another publication, we wouldn't get paid by the *New Zealand Woman's Weekly* and we wouldn't be able to pay for the wedding we'd just had!

I was beside myself with worry. It took several of our other guests – one of them a lawyer – to talk the would-be photographer out of it. It was a huge relief when all the magazines came out the following week and only the official photos appeared in the *Woman's Weekly*.

After the excitement of the wedding, we went back to doing promotional work for the direct marketing company which had asked me to endorse their make-up. Unfortunately the arrangement we had with this company didn't work out and once again I found myself almost penniless, despite all our hard work and my best intentions.

> I think people got the impression, because I was on TV all the time selling stuff, I was making a fortune and keeping it all for myself.

When you've lost everything and have to start again from scratch, to feel safe and secure the things you need most are stability and peace of mind. I needed regular money coming in, I needed to be able to save and to budget to pay bills. I hated seeing Duncan get upset when his kids had their birthdays and we couldn't afford to send them anything. He worried they'd think it meant he didn't care and had forgotten about them.

On a long-term basis, you can't live with the constant fear and panic of not knowing where your next penny is coming from or when it is likely to arrive. The uncertainty caused me to worry all the time.

Because I'd promised on national television to repay all my creditors, the newspapers were ringing me from time to time to find out why I hadn't paid up yet. It was stressful having to answer questions everywhere I went about why I wasn't paying people back. Screaming, 'Because I don't have the money,' didn't help matters in the slightest. I think people got the impression, because I was on TV all the time selling stuff, I was making a fortune and keeping it all for myself. Things couldn't have been further from the truth.

It was hard going out into the malls day after day. It really wasn't my passion anymore. I found it incredibly hard work and it took such a lot of energy to fake it every day.

How did my life get into such a mess? I've always wanted to do the right thing and I've always believed if you're honest and work hard things will come right. This time they couldn't have been more wrong.

I'd love to be able to tell you that the next day I leapt out of bed full of energy and motivation to start all over again from nothing, but I didn't. I felt like a sledgehammer had knocked all the life out of me. I felt old and drained and completely worn out. We only had fifty-three dollars in the bank. I'd had enough. I didn't have the energy anymore, I was too old.

Writing this book gave me the motivation to pick myself up and try again. I'd been jotting down notes all year and, surely, if I put them all together and took my own advice I'd be able to give things another go. I felt a bit of a fraud writing a motivational book. Surely I should feel on top of the world and full of life and enthusiasm to write a motivational book — not feel ready to throw myself off the Harbour Bridge. But, just maybe, that was the best time to start writing it — when I was so low and miserable that most things seemed hopeless . . . if the steps were going to work for me now, they'd work for everybody.

So, I started putting into practice every lesson I'd learned over the years. Within the month I received a phone call asking if I would like to take part in filming an episode of the TV show *Intrepid Journeys* in Sri Lanka. It would mean three and a half weeks away in November.

I didn't want to be away from Duncan and Mum for so long,

> It's not the spectacular scenery I remember most about the journey now, but the joy of the people who you might think had nothing to be happy about.

especially as it coincided with my fiftieth birthday. But I had been wishing I could be somewhere exotic for my birthday and I really wanted to present the episode. I thought if I reminded the TV bosses of what I could do, I might get some more work. The show didn't pay much, but when the producers agreed to fly Duncan in for my birthday I agreed to go. I was disappointed when I got a call to say the trip had been cancelled because it was too dangerous to travel in the area – Tamils were attacking visitors there.

However, I was asked to travel from Hanoi to Hong Kong instead, if I wanted to. I agreed and what a great adventure it turned out to be.

It was a small crew – just the director, cameraman, production manager and me. I sobbed uncontrollably when I had to leave Duncan – we hated being apart even for a single day. I didn't know how I was going to survive for three weeks.

Hanoi must surely be the noisiest place in the world. I was staying in backpacker-style accommodation right in the heart of the city and the noise level never changed – it remained constant twenty-four hours a day. I never got a wink of sleep. Apart from the traffic, there was always karaoke blaring out at an ear-splitting volume. None of the singers could carry a tune in a bucket and I was glad we were only there a couple of nights.

I spent several days travelling through Vietnam on a variety of rickety old buses staying in small villages and sampling the traditional way of life.

A highlight of the journey was meeting the old soldier at the underground hospital. He must have been eighty if he was a day and he'd been standing guard there for fifty years.

Now, it was his job now to escort visitors through the maze of rooms carved into the hillside, stopping only to sing a hauntingly beautiful song in a voice still strong and clear. He looked so happy and proud. I don't know what the song was about but it sounded so sad, I wanted to give him a hug. So I did.

The endless travelling was a nightmare. Some of the buses were such boneshakers I couldn't even hold a book steady to read. Live pigs ran about and chickens flapped all over me. People were throwing up – it was madness. The squat-toilets at the bus stations were a nightmare. I went into one and came straight out again. I had a guide with me to make sure I got on the right bus and she said, 'Make sure you go to the toilet now, because if you think that one is bad, the next bus station is worse.' I took her word for it and went straight back in. There were no walls or doors, and all I could see was the side view of all these women in a row doing their ablutions over a long drain. I was retching as I squatted over the drain, as everything flowed past me and splashed up my legs. The smell was evil and I just wanted to go home and have a hot shower. Instead, I got on another bus that nearly shook the brains right out of my head.

We crossed the border into rural China and travelled for three days towards the Long Ji, staying with the hill-tribe communities. It's not the spectacular scenery I remember most about the journey now, but the joy of the people who you might think had nothing to be happy about. Even though they had very little, strangers invited me into their homes to share a bowl of rice and a cup of tea – I use the word tea loosely. I assumed as they were living in extreme poverty that people would be miserable, but they were laughing and joking, always pleased to be with family and friends. They didn't care if they

BE MORE AFRAID OF
REGRET THAN FAILURE

didn't have electricity. They were quite content and for me it was quite humbling.

One of the hardest challenges was the hike up through the Long Ji rice terraces to reach my accommodation at the top. At sixty-six square kilometres, Long Ji is one of the world's largest and most beautiful rice terraces. I had a toothless old granny as my guide and felt old and unfit as she charged ahead, carrying my bag! She didn't speak a word of English and after four hours I started to worry that she didn't know where she was going. Even if she did, I feared that I wasn't going to make it. I didn't know if it would take another four hours or if we'd be there in ten minutes. I started to panic. It's always the not-knowing that makes a situation worse. I can cope with anything as long as I know what's coming.

In the end, it took just over five hours to get to the top and I collapsed in a heap, while super-granny had a bowl of rice before setting off back down to the bottom!

The night before my birthday I arrived in Yangshao, China. Duncan was due the next day. I was just getting ready for bed, when there was a knock at the door. I was a bit nervous and wouldn't open it. 'Who is it?' I demanded. I couldn't understand the reply, so said again, 'Who is it?' 'It's your husband,' came the reply. I don't think I've ever been so pleased to see someone in my entire life. The production team had flown him in a day early to surprise me.

On my fiftieth birthday I had acupuncture, learnt kung fu from an old master named Papa and ate chips and gravy in a café as a special treat. I had a wonderful day. I wouldn't have cared where I was, as long as Duncan was with me.

My intrepid journey ended in Hong Kong and even though I knew that being happy didn't have anything to do with having possessions, it didn't stop me wishing I had the money to shop up a storm at Stanley Market.

Back home, I made new plans and started taking small steps.

Little did I know that on my return from China a phone call would change my life forever and that some of my wildest dreams would come true.

Act like an ostrich

To move forward you may have to change the way you do things, at least for a while.

After Rawaka closed, if ever I had to drive over the Harbour Bridge I would make sure I was in the right-hand lane, so I didn't have to see Fishermans Wharf. The sight of it would upset me and ruin the rest of my day.

When I had to move out of my dream home on the cliff, I couldn't go and visit some very good friends of mine for about a year – their house overlooked what had been mine and I couldn't bear to look over it and see new owners. My friends understood and kept asking me around for dinner until one day I realised I was strong enough to handle it, and I accepted the invitation.

I still don't drive over the Harbour Bridge in the left-hand lane heading north, but I'll know when I can.

Time flies

Some things you can never get back. Time is one of them. I was angry when I felt as if I had wasted three years of my life that I would never get back. When you're young, you think you have all the time in the world to achieve your dreams. As you get older, you panic that there won't be enough time left to do everything you want or need to do.

When men feel like this they call it a mid-life crisis.

Failure is another part of the journey.

> I found out that, just as success isn't a destination but only part of the journey, so failure is another part of the journey. The journey doesn't end until you die.

When you're going through hell, keep going!

Standing in the malls with my performance – happy – face on, people used to come up to me every day saying things like, 'You're so strong. I couldn't start again', and 'I'm not brave like you. I wouldn't be able to cope' and 'It's easier for you. I can't handle stress.'

Instead of making me feel better, their comments made me feel like screaming. Did they think I was some sort of unfeeling robot who didn't have the same emotions as them? I wanted to shout out, 'I'm in pain, too. I'd rather stay at home as well and do nothing.'

But then I realised they just didn't know how to start again. They didn't know where to start and what steps to take.

I knew because I'd tried more things and I'd failed at more things.

I'd learnt lessons along the way and I knew what I had to do to pick myself up.

I knew how I had to think and how I had to feel.

I also knew I had to write it all down, so that everyone else would know.

Notes

13

Put a smile on your dial

At the end of January 2007, my agent rang to tell me that I'd been picked to appear in the third series of *Dancing with the Stars*. It sounded too good to be true. I kept saying, 'No, are you sure? No, really? No. Are you sure?' Karen assured me I'd be getting a contract any day soon and I thought I would explode with sheer joy. I burst into tears. Duncan came running at all the noise I was making and soon we were both laughing and dancing round the room. It was the most wonderful, exciting feeling I've ever had. Soon Mum had joined in, and we were all talking at once, wondering about who else would be in the show, who my dance partner would be and what the costumes would look like. I couldn't sleep that night – I was buzzing with energy and I felt alive again.

I was bursting to tell everyone but it had to be kept top secret until rehearsals started in a month's time. I had to come clean with my brothers, however, because I was laughing and grinning like something demented and they wanted to know why.

I was really excited when it was time for the meet-and-greet party at the Heritage Hotel in Auckland. I couldn't wait to find out who the other celebrities were and to meet my dance partner, Stefano Olivieri. I'd seen a photo of him, so I knew who I was looking for. I also knew he was coming over from Australia and had won several championships.

What I didn't know was how tall he was. At six foot two inches high, he towered a good head and shoulders above me! I'm sure he must have thought he'd drawn the short straw with me. I thought we'd look rather comical tripping the light fantastic.

At the age of fifty, I was the oldest female in the show, but I promised Stefano I was going to give it my best shot and wouldn't let him down. We started rehearsals the next day at City Dance, on Auckland's Queen Street.

When I take on a new challenge, my personality means it becomes all-consuming, leaving no time for anything else. Duncan and I agreed that he would take over the day-to-day running of the home, including shopping and cooking, as well as all our business activities. We'd been working on a whole new range of beauty products as well as looking for a business partner and fundraising. It was going to be a busy time for him, but it was the only way I could put the necessary hours in to do well.

I was up against the actress Greer Robson again. She'd won *Celebrity Treasure Island* the year I was on it. I knew she was a tough little thing who liked to win. But after feeling like a loser for so long, I was determined to give her a run for her money. Stefano had six weeks to turn a middle-aged woman into a dancing queen. He certainly had his work cut out. I'd done my bit of ballet and tap at the local church hall as a kid, but that had been thirty-five years ago and I hadn't been very good then.

Our first dance was the cha-cha followed by the quickstep. Both are very fast dances that had me sweating and gasping for breath in minutes. The tiny dance studio was in a very old building, so there was no air-conditioning and the humidity and heat were stifling. I was constantly fanning myself or lying down with a wet flannel on my head between dances.

Although we were only required to put in two hours a day practice, there's nothing stopping you if you want to do more. Stefano didn't have any other commitments in New Zealand so we decided we would do as much as possible, dancing six, seven and, sometimes, eight hours a day until I could barely stand up and my feet were so swollen and blistered I couldn't get my shoes on.

Every night I would get home, completely shattered and lie on the couch with my legs up in the air while Duncan, bless him, massaged my feet. Then I'd get up and spend the night going round and round the kitchen floor . . . two three cha-cha-cha, two three cha-cha-cha.

After a couple of weeks I tore a muscle in my leg and it went completely black from the thigh to the knee. Then I bruised my ribs while attempting some tricky lifts. People kept saying, 'You're on the dancing show – you must be so fit now'. The truth was most days, I just felt fit to drop.

But, for the first time in years, I wasn't worrying about money. I didn't have all the stress of juggling finances, paying bills and robbing Peter to pay Paul. But I felt guilty about leaving Duncan at home to cope with it all. I threw myself into dancing one hundred per cent and didn't think about anything else. It was a wonderful escape from the reality of day-to-day and I loved every minute.

Stefano and I had such fun and laughed every day that I was starting to feel like my old self again – full of life and energy. So that we would always remember the wonderful experience, we got matching star tattoos. Mine is at the top of my thigh and Stefano's is on his chest.

By the end of the six weeks I was better than I thought I'd be, thanks to Stefano's patience and dedication. We couldn't wait to see how all the other competitors were doing. We practised at different studios so none of us had any idea how we compared to anyone else. I just hoped I didn't make a complete fool of myself in front of the whole nation.

The show went to air live every Tuesday night and for the first week of the series we had to arrive in Wellington on the Sunday morning to begin rehearsing. It was being filmed at Avalon studios, where they also film the *Good Morning* show. It was great catching up with everyone again, hearing all the gossip and checking out the studio. I couldn't believe how little the dance floor looked and we spent hours that first day rehearsing the basic elements of the show – where we had to stand, when we had to come down the stairs, when to go over and talk to the host, Jason Gunn, and when we should walk over to Candy Lane's grotto. Everything needed to be perfectly timed so that the live show looked slick and polished.

On the Monday morning, I had a mini-meltdown and poor Stefano didn't know what to say or do for the best, so he didn't do anything. There were four couples doing the cha-cha and when I saw how young and gorgeous the other girls looked in their fabulous costumes, I suddenly felt like an old frump. It wasn't the outfit – on anyone else I'm sure it would have looked divine. It was me. Who did I think I was trying to kid? I was going to look ridiculous in anything. I could practically see the headlines now: 'Talk about mutton dressed as lamb'. I was going to be the laughing stock of the whole country. I locked myself in the toilet and wouldn't come out. I was horrified to think that I was about to make a complete show of myself on nationwide television and embarrass Duncan into the bargain! I cried and cried and wondered what the hell I'd been thinking.

> Stefano couldn't believe the change in me overnight. I'd gone from a blubbering wreck to someone strong and calm and very determined to go out there and knock their socks off!

Eventually, I had to come out and the other dancers tried to consol me. But saying 'You look great for your age' didn't help. I didn't want to be my age – that was the problem. I wanted to be their age. That's what nobody had told me about growing old. Even when you're fifty you still feel twenty. It's when you look in the mirror and think, 'Dear God, who's that with my clothes on?' that it hits home. I'd forgotten I wasn't a sexy young thing anymore, but the reality was staring straight back at me and I wanted to go home.

Sharon, the head make-up artist, tried to cheer me up and so did Debs the producer. The kinder they were the more I cried. In the end it was the lovely Lorraine Downes that coaxed me back onto the set. 'Forget about everyone else,' said the former Miss Universe, who had won *Dancing with the Stars* the previous year. 'It's not about them. Don't worry about what they're doing, just concentrate on yourself and think about your performance. As long as you're out there enjoying yourself, then the public will, too.'

Back at the hotel that night I had a word with myself. I'd waited three years to be invited on the show and couldn't throw it all away now. So I was no spring chicken, but I could still go out there and dance with all my heart and soul and make Mum and Duncan proud.

Stefano couldn't believe the change in me overnight. I'd gone from a blubbering wreck to someone strong and calm and very determined to go out there and knock their socks off!

My confidence soared when our wonderful wardrobe lady, Claire, came at me with a pair of scissors and cut the bottom off my dress to reveal lots of leg. That surprised a lot of people, including me.

Stefano and I were the first couple to dance and, even though it was nerve-racking to open the show, I was glad to get it out of the way so I could start to relax. Mum wasn't well enough to travel so I said 'Hello, Mum' on screen to her sitting at home and I felt a rush of adrenaline when I heard the words, 'Will Suzanne Paul and Stefano Olivieri please take to the floor!'

The crowd went wild as we cha-cha'd for all we were worth. Seeing Duncan sitting in the front row looking so proud and happy made my heart soar. It was the longest one and a half minutes of my whole life and I enjoyed every second! I hadn't fallen down the stairs or forgotten the steps or made an idiot of myself. I'd done it and I felt on top of the world. If I could have bottled and sold that feeling right there and then, I would have been a millionaire again in no time.

That night, Stefano and I got the second-highest score behind singer Megan Alatini and her partner Jonny Williams. I was just thrilled to have got through the dance – everything after that was a bonus.

Later that night at the after party, we all watched the show on a huge screen. It was the first time we'd all seen ourselves perform and it was the last time for me. How I thought I looked and how I saw it on the screen were two different things and I didn't like what I saw. I decided if it was going to make me self-conscious, I wouldn't watch myself anymore. That way I wouldn't worry what I looked like. It worked for me.

On the Wednesday morning we flew back to Auckland to start practising for the quickstep and, just in case we survived the second elimination, I also learnt a bit of the jive routine. I think the quickstep is one of the funniest dances and I usually got a fit of the giggles as I charged round the floor with my little legs going like the clappers to keep up with Stefano's big long ones.

Talking about legs, so was the whole country by all accounts. Everywhere I went people commented on my shapely legs and couldn't believe they belonged to a fifty-year-old woman. It did wonders for my ego, I must say. It was just what I needed.

We came second again that week and I was thrilled to know my charity, Starship Childrens Hospital, would be earning money from our votes. Stefano and I visited some of the children in hospital and did a special dance for them. The money we raised would be used to buy more incubators for premature babies, so we popped up to the neonatal unit to have a look around.

As we walked past one of the incubators I said to Stefano, 'There's no baby in that one.' A nurse called me back and said, 'Yes, there's baby Melody in here.' She was so tiny, like a little scrap of baby bird, right in the middle of this huge machine, that both Stefano and I had tears running down our faces at the sight of this precious little girl fighting for her life. It didn't look possible for her to survive, but she did.

Life became a whirlwind of photo shoots and dancing, publicity and interviews and, apart from the pain, I was having a marvellous time. With three fast dances in a row and the constant lifting and throwing, I'd cracked one of my ribs at the back. The doctor said nothing could be done except to rest it for a few weeks. He also said if I carried on dancing it could break and puncture a lung – lovely!

I had a meeting with the producer. Debs was concerned that I would do myself even more damage should I continue. She had fought hard to get me on the show and I would be forever grateful, so I assured her that I wanted to carry on and that it was my own responsibility. If something were to go wrong, I wouldn't hold TVNZ accountable.

Mother Nature can be so cruel. Just when you get your head together, your body falls apart. But Stefano and I managed to survive another week; coming first with the judges for our jive, I was on cloud nine.

The best thing about our dance studio was the location right above McDonald's, which meant I could have my favourite – a quarter pounder, medium fries and a small cup of tea – for lunch every day. I figured this would be the only time in my life when I could eat what I wanted and not gain weight. At night Duncan cooked me wonderful, healthy food and I still managed to lose about four kilograms. As for Stefano, he never stops eating and you'd find more meat on a butcher's pencil!

In episode four we did the foxtrot, which I wasn't confident about. I'd become used to charging about every week and only had two speeds – fast and very fast. The foxtrot seemed unbearably slow and I thought I looked like Groucho Marx lolloping about. The height difference also meant Stefano and I had trouble dancing close together in the ballroom section and, even though we lost points for that, we managed to survive another elimination round.

The following week we stepped up rehearsals even more. We had to do two dances, a swing waltz, which was done as a group, and the samba. For this, Claire and the team had made me a gorgeous pink-and-orange frilly number and it was a lively and fun dance to do. I was chuffed to bits when we came second.

The competition was getting harder and every day was filled with trying to remember to do everything all at once. It seemed as if, when my legs were right my arms were all wrong and if my arms were right my head was all over the place. Even my eyes had to be looking in the right direction! I used to get so frustrated and angry with myself when I couldn't master a certain step that we would go over and over the same thing for hours on end until I nearly went doolally.

I didn't lose my temper with Stefano until we were doing the rhumba in week six. I just couldn't get into the mood of the dance. I'd feel like a right fool at ten o'clock in the morning with Stefano saying, 'Walk sexy and run your hands over your body. Now look at me as though you want me.' I would shout at him, 'I can't do it. I think I look like an idiot,' and he would just shout back, 'Don't think. Just do it!'

So I did it. But I was dreading the judges' reaction. I wasn't surprised when Craig Revell-Horward joked we looked like an old married couple who were getting a divorce! I was so mad at their cruel comments that when we came out later to do the tango I was all fired up with anger. I looked daggers at the judges and thought, 'I'll show you who can dance with passion.' I threw myself into it, body and soul, and the crowd went wild. We survived another week!

I couldn't believe I was through to the semi-finals and Stefano was looking forward to doing the waltz – it was one of his favourite dances. He choreographed the most beautiful routine and I knew if we could pull it off there wouldn't be a dry eye in the house – it was so lovely and romantic.

Only seconds into the routine, the back of my dress became entangled in the microphone attached to Stefano's lapel. As

I turned to face him the wire wrapped around my body and I could hardly move one way or the other. Through my smile I whispered to him, 'I'm stuck.' Through an even bigger smile he said, 'I know. I know. Just keep keeping going.'

We couldn't do the routine properly and I had a look of sheer terror on my face as I kept trying to pull the microphone off me, but it wouldn't budge.

We'd been told early on in the series, that there were only two reasons you were allowed to stop during a dance. One was if your heel fell off and the other was if you had a wardrobe malfunction, à la Janet Jackson, and exposed one or more of your boobs. So we carried on.

The judges awarded us the lowest score of the night, saying what had happened was unfortunate and bad luck, but that was life. When we went backstage, I was angry and upset, thinking we were probably going to be eliminated for something that wasn't our fault. The producer came to see me and told me not to give up just yet. We still had one more dance to do and people were phoning in and voting for us.

So we changed into our paso doble outfits and Claire had really outdone herself this time. We were dancing to the *Mission Impossible* theme and were both dressed as secret agents. Stefano had come up with the designs. I was in a long black leather skirt with splits up to the thigh and Stefano in a long leather coat that he swirled about him like a cape. I was hardly recognisable in my black bob wig and bright red lipstick. The crowd roared when we strode out onto the floor. It was an exciting and fiery routine and we'd never danced it better. At one point Stefano had to grab me around the middle, throw me into the air and hold me high above his head. It was such a difficult move, and most of the time in training I ended up on the floor or doubled over in pain from my ribs, but we knew if we could master it on the night we'd bring the house down. We went for it. As I whirled above Stefano's head I wanted to shout out, 'I did it, look at me!'

The judges loved it, apart from Brendan Cole who thought it was gimmicky, causing me to lose my temper and give him some backchat. Never mind, we were through to the final!

For the last week of training, Stefano and I practised up to ten hours a day. We had to perform three dances and the pressure was really on. I hadn't been getting much sleep because I was unable to lie down with the pain in my rib and had to try and sleep sitting up. I was totally exhausted and didn't know how I was going to get through the next few days.

I tried some really strong painkillers one day, but I couldn't remember the routines. All I could hear was Stefano saying, 'What are you doing? Why are you going over there? Where are your arms supposed to be?' I felt as if everything was in slow motion. As usual, Duncan was there to support me, and my brother Bill had also come along with his fiancée. I didn't want them to see how much pain I was in, because they'd have been worried.

Our first dance was the cha-cha and as I leapt into Stefano's arms, I felt a sharp pain in my side, like being stabbed with a knife. Stefano had to dip me over backwards then pull me up again, and as he did so, he heard 'Aaaaaaahhhhhhhhh!' in his ear. We still wore huge smiles on our faces as he said, 'Are you okay?' and I replied, 'Just carry on!'

I was afraid to take deep breaths in case I did any internal damage, plus it was too painful. I was panting like a dog when we went over for our chat with Jason.

When I got backstage to get changed into my next outfit, there were two physiotherapists on hand to look after me. They sprayed ice onto the area and taped me up as best they could. All the while, the floor manager was speaking into his headphones, saying, 'I don't think she's going on, the rib's given out. She can't go on.'

There was no way I was giving in now. I thought it was better that I collapsed out on the dance floor than not go on, but I couldn't even undress myself. Two wardrobe ladies stripped me and put me in my dress for the tango. They even had to fasten my shoes for me, too. I wasn't sure how far into the dance I would get, but told Stefano I wanted to give it my best shot. I just hoped that when the music started, the adrenaline would kick in and I could block out the pain.

It wasn't the best tango I've ever done and afterwards I could barely move. Stefano had to push my legs forward with his legs so I could walk over to Jason and the judges. After two dances Megan and Jonny were in the lead.

For the final dance, both couples had to do a freestyle dance, meaning we could pretty much do whatever we liked. We'd chosen a medley from *West Side Story*, which started slow with lots of wonderful lifts then my dress was ripped off to reveal a sexy red-and-black number underneath. The end was fast and furious with us both charging about the stage. To finish I leapt onto Stefano's shoulder. To this day I don't know how I got up there. We got a near-perfect score of thirty-nine and went into the lead.

Now we just had to find out how the public had voted. Standing there next to Stefano I felt like we were the only people in the room. You could have heard a pin drop. My heart was pounding and I kept saying my own name over and over in my head, willing Jason to say it as well. Stefano and I looked absolutely terrified as we waited and waited.

When I heard my name I screamed and was so overcome with emotion I burst into tears. It was one of the happiest days of my life. I was a winner again.

Where there's a will there's a way

I don't think I was a better dancer than all the others, but I think the public could see how much it meant to me to win, and they wanted me to win.

Every week they could see the determination I had and they could tell that I was giving it everything, and then some.

I didn't hold back. Every emotion was right there for them to share – good and bad. I never had to pretend I was enjoying myself or dance with a fake smile on my face. I danced with feeling and passion. Because it was real they all came along for the ride.

It became more than just a dance competition. People who had also failed and hit rock bottom wanted me to succeed, because it meant that they could, too.

Don't worry, be happy

Every morning when you get up, say to yourself, 'I'm going to be happy today.' You have to take responsibility for your own happiness – tell yourself to be happy.

Stefano and other people like him are a joy to be around because they spread happiness wherever they go. They smile at people and people smile back.

Every morning when
you get up, say to
yourself, 'I'm going
to be happy today.'

Whatever you give out, you get back

If you're not happy in your work then either stop and find a job that you love, or look for some other way to bring happiness into your life. It might be a hobby, a pet or spending more time with your children.

Life shouldn't feel like a job – it's supposed to be fun.
You should be having a good time!

A lot of people set aside occasions when they allow themselves to have fun and are miserable the rest of the time. They just go about working, watching TV, paying bills and being busy, looking forward to their two weeks' holiday in December when they're going to enjoy themselves. For others, Monday to Friday is for serious stuff and laughing is only to be done on a weekend.

The best things in life are free

Choose to be happy every day and try and find joy in the little things around you. Treasure every moment you have with loved ones.

Last year we rediscovered the joy of butterflies when Duncan put a swan plant in the garden. Mum and I watched the circle of life, transfixed as each caterpillar turned into a chrysalis that sparkled with gold jewels, then amazed two weeks later when each beautiful monarch butterfly emerged, its damp wings drying in the breeze. We both cheered as the butterflies took their maiden flights!

Notes

14

Next week's fish 'n' chip paper

Everywhere I went people were congratulating me. I had to laugh one day when a little girl said, 'Everyone in my class voted for you, even though you're really old.' I thought it was hilarious but her mother looked horrified.

It was nice to have people stop and chat about something happy and positive for a change. Even the newspapers were writing nice things, although they couldn't resist mentioning on the night of the *Dancing with the Stars* final that I hadn't paid all the creditors back yet. They didn't mention that Duncan and

I didn't even have a car between us!

At least I knew things were beginning to change, just not as fast as I wanted them to. I was on such a high after *Dancing with the Stars* that I went straight to the top of TVNZ and asked what sort of show they'd like me to present.

How about a game show? A chat show? A dating game? Anything?

Nothing.

I must admit I was a bit surprised, though it's probably my own fault for reading too many women's magazines. In England after winning – or even coming second or third – people were offered their own TV shows to cash in on their current popularity, plus they are offered all sorts of fitness videos and endorsements for biscuits or shoes or McDonald's. I'd been expecting a similar sort of reaction here. But there was nothing offered.

So I moved on to plan B, which was to come up with an idea for a TV show that would be so fabulous the bosses at TVNZ would not be able to resist it. Part two of plan B was to make some phone calls to see who'd like me to endorse their products. No one did. Never mind, I just had to keep saying to myself that someone wanted me to promote their products and they were on their way to me. I wished they'd hurry up.

For six months Duncan and I had been working on my dream of getting Natural Glow back into the market. After Paul and I sold Prestige Marketing it kept going for a few years until the company went into liquidation. Natural Glow was no more. Ever since, women kept saying to me they couldn't live without their Natural Glow. I was often asked if I could bring it back.

There was also a lot of confusion in the market – people thought every bronzing powder was mine. It was no wonder the media thought I had money flowing in. After a while I realised

> *I realised that if I could relaunch Natural Glow people might stop buying the copies and go back to the original.*

that if I could relaunch Natural Glow people might stop buying the copies and go back to the original. From then on all I could think about was getting my beloved Natural Glow back on the market, but that was not as easy to achieve as it sounds.

We'd found a liquidator's report on the internet showing who owned the rights to it now, and after several phone calls to the States we managed to talk them into selling the rights to me. They knew I had invented it and could see it was an opportunity to make some money from the name.

Now, all we needed was the cash to buy the name back.

Raising funds, whether you're looking for investors or looking for partners, is one of the most soul-destroying things you can do. Every day you're out there trying, your confidence is chipped away bit by bit until there's hardly any left.

I'd thought the pairing of the names Natural Glow and Suzanne Paul would have people knocking on the door wanting to be a part of it. Didn't my previous success count for anything? Apparently not. Every day we went out knocking on doors, meeting with strangers, making business plans, showing marketing plans, waiting for phone calls. As always, the waiting was the worst.

And just when we started to think things were okay they would all fall apart and we'd be back to square one, with nothing.

I felt the stigma of being a former bankrupt was following me. Is that how I would be judged from now on?

But you have to keep the faith – you have to believe you're

one step closer to the person who will say yes even when everyone around you is saying 'no, no, no'. I spent months working on new and innovative products that I could launch under the Natural Glow banner and my brother Bill designed packaging and new logos for them. We'd got as far as we could with no money and were trying to keep the guys in the States happy with promises that it was all happening and money would be forthcoming. Again, I wished it would hurry up.

In July I had a meeting with a team from Postie Plus to discuss the idea of a clothing range with my name on it in their stores. I was beside myself with excitement. This was exactly what I'd been waiting for.

Several meetings later I went to Christchurch to meet with the buyer and to select the clothes from that season's range that I would be happy to put my name to. Over the next month, I also did some motivational speaking to their staff and made a sales-training video. Things were looking up. We still hadn't found an investor for Natural Glow, but we were in discussions with a group of businessmen who were willing to put in a certain amount each and we were working on a contract for that.

One thing that had picked up since my success in *Dancing with the Stars* was the number of motivational speaking engagements I was getting. At the height of my previous success, I used to get regular bookings and would travel all over the country extolling the virtues of 'never giving up' and 'having another go'. But, of course, all that dried up with my well-publicised failure. Now I was in demand again for my picking-yourself-back-up talks and although it's still not something I'm crazy about doing, at least it kept the wolf from the door most days.

Postie Plus had kindly given me some of the clothes from my new range due to hit stores the following summer, so I was keen to start promoting them whenever I could. I went to several high-profile events wearing the clothes, telling anyone that would listen about my new range. I even wore some of them to a Trelise Cooper fashion show. I thought it very amusing when I came out and the runway reporter asked us all where our outfits were from. You could hear well-dressed women saying 'Gucci', 'Armani' and 'Chanel'. When it was my turn I was grinning from ear to ear as I said 'Postie Plus'. I looked pretty good and felt good, too!

My whole world was turned upside down at the end of September, when the *Sunday Star-Times* reported that I was being sued by a direct-marketing company. The reporter had received the information about it before I did!

All I could think was that someone had fed the story to the paper to stop me raising the funds to relaunch Natural Glow – they didn't want me as their competition and had decided to resort to dirty tactics to stop me. It worked.

My potential investors pulled out, and a couple of weeks later I received a letter from Postie Plus to say the clothing-label deal was off, because of the negative publicity. Four months of work for nothing, except a couple of nice outfits!

A couple of weeks later there was another story in the papers asking why I hadn't paid the creditors back. Hello. Why didn't they ask me? I could have told them exactly why – because the story they'd printed had stopped me from earning the money to do so! How was I going to be able to pay back anybody at this rate?

I was taking three steps forward and six back. As low as I felt, I had to keep going – keep things moving, keep trying. Get up every day and have another go. Knowing what you have to do to succeed doesn't make it any easier. You still doubt yourself, still say 'Why me? Life isn't fair!'

But knowing what I have to do helps me get back on the horse quicker. Instead of wallowing about in self-pity for months or weeks, I put into practice everything I'm writing about.

I'd thought of quite a few ideas for TV shows, but it wasn't until October that I knew I was onto a winner and went along again to TVNZ to see what they thought. The whole world seemed to be going dance crazy and I'd come up with a dancing show I called 'Ballroom Blitz'. It would make for great viewing. The guy I had to see loved the idea and we both agreed it would make a great TV One show – something the whole family could sit down to watch together on a Sunday night.

I was advised to find a production company who would be able to put it together for me as a proper proposal with a timeframe and costings. I went away the happiest person on the planet.

In terms of relaunching Natural Glow, the guys in the States were getting itchy feet with all the promises. It'd been nearly a year since we asked to buy the name from them and we still hadn't come up with a cent.

A good friend of ours had been helping us with the business plan and he had a small amount he was prepared to invest with us in return for a shareholding in the company. It meant we were able to order stock and send a part payment to the States. The ball was rolling, the ads were all written and ready to be filmed and we'd arranged distribution and warehousing.

We just needed that one big investor who would have a bit of faith in us. He arrived towards the end of November and I thanked God and the universe for sending him to me at last. Natural Glow hit the stores in late December and we were off.

It was a different Christmas for us that year. It was the first year we'd been allowed to have Duncan's three children to stay. Not really children any more, the twins Hamish and Rachael were seventeen and Zoe had just turned fifteen. Together, we all did a lovely feel-good story for a women's magazine. I didn't stop to think about the repercussions from the headline, 'Suzanne becomes a mum at last'. I soon found out when I went to collect a copy of the magazine and the lady behind the counter said, 'Congratulations.' She looked at me a bit strangely when I replied, 'Thank you, Stefano was a lovely lad. We had a lot of fun.' It wasn't until I was leaving the shop and another lady said the same, and started rubbing my tummy, that I realised they weren't congratulating me for winning the dancing – everybody thought I was pregnant! I had about a month of that and I don't know who was more embarrassed – me or the people doing the congratulating.

On Christmas Day Duncan and I went along to the City Mission to help with the Christmas dinner. They have a few hundred people turn up and they ask celebrities to pop along for an hour to help entertain them. Christmas can be a lonely time for many people and I wanted to go along and just try to make the day a bit special for them. It was also a reminder that there were many people worse off than me. I was thankful to be able to share Christmas with wonderful family and friends later. It didn't matter if I wasn't able to buy them all fancy presents anymore, we were all together and that's what mattered.

I love New Year. I love having a good clearout and getting rid of any clutter and clothes that haven't been worn for a while. Mum and Duncan dread seeing me with pink collection bags – I'm ruthless at throwing things away. It's just such a good feeling afterwards to see clean and

> I realised they weren't congratulating me for winning the dancing – everybody thought I was pregnant!

tidy cupboards and drawers. I don't know why, but I feel in control and ready for anything when things are in order. I can't stand mess.

New Year is also a great time to start a journal. The year ahead seems so long and full of promise, I can't wait to write down all my new plans. It's also good to look back and see what I've achieved over the previous year. It helps to keep me motivated to keep on making big plans and taking small steps.

After my last meeting with TVNZ I'd been to see Greenstone Pictures about helping me develop 'Ballroom Blitz'. They had filmed most of my other shows, including *Guess Who's Coming to Dinner*. I was confident they'd make a great job of the proposal.

We had a few meetings and they loved my ideas, and they had a few of their own to make the show even better. They needed to work on the proposal, which would take a few months, before they could present it again to the network. We were all very excited, especially as the new series of *Dancing with the Stars* was about to begin and it was all anyone could talk about. It was proof that dancing shows were still popular. What better way to follow it than with a new dancing show?

It didn't seem possible that it was already time for me to perform with Stefano again, this time as last year's winners. I felt quite guilty because I didn't have any of the stress of the competition – I could just go out there and enjoy myself – while the new group of celebrities were bags of nerves.

We were the opening act. I loved every moment of our jive and I was sorry when it came to and end. I knew I wouldn't get the chance to perform again in front of an audience. I'd had my turn. Now it was time for others to shine. I was thrilled when Stefano and his new dance partner, netballer Temepara George, got the highest marks of the night. I knew she was in for a wonderful journey over the next few weeks and it would be strange sitting at home watching it on the telly.

It hadn't been plain sailing getting the new Natural Glow into pharmacies, but we were picking up speed every week and more and more were coming on board. One of the problems was the other bronzers on the market. I had secret shoppers going into stores asking for Natural Glow and very often they were sold something completely different. Women were saying they'd just bought my new Natural Glow, only to produce something else from their bag. It was driving me mad.

We decided to have a stand at Girls' Day Out, which was held over three days in March. It seemed like a wonderful opportunity to talk to a lot of women and demonstrate the product. They generally get around forty-five thousand women over the three days. Hopefully, we'd make lots of sales. There'd be eight of us on the stand demonstrating the product, including my regular demonstrator – Khadija was a real firecracker who'd worked for me off and on for years. Duncan and Chap, our friend and shareholder, were also going to be there to complete the sales and do the eftpos transactions.

A couple of days before Girls' Day Out, I had a call from Greenstone Pictures to say that, after months of thinking about it, TVNZ decided they didn't have enough money in the budget to go ahead with 'Ballroom Blitz'. I was absolutely devastated. I had convinced myself it was going to be the next big hit. I hadn't expected them to turn it down and couldn't believe it. My dreams of a new TV show were shattered, once again.

The last thing I felt like doing was chatting and laughing with thousands of women, but life must go on. Anyway, it was better that I was busy so I wouldn't have time to dwell on it. As soon as the Girls' Day Out opened at 10 am on the Friday we were flat out, dusting and demonstrating like madwomen. It was tiring but fun, and the young girls queued to have their photos taken with me or to get an autograph.

Other bronzers were also being demonstrated and sold at the show, but I was confident of my product and the marketing campaign I'd done, so I wasn't worried about the competition or what they were doing.

Every day for an hour, Duncan and I went up onto the cookery stage, as the celebrity chefs. I did all the talking and Duncan did all the cooking. In exchange we got a discount off the fee for our stand, so we didn't mind. We did the same meal every day – a sort of Kiwi version of a traditional Lancashire hotpot. Afterwards it was back to the stand for more selling and I was worn out by the time we got home at about 7.30 pm each night.

Saturday was pretty much the same except it was twice as busy. By then I was looking forward to the Sunday as it was the last day and I was already exhausted.

The next day, the *Sunday Star-Times* did a really annoying story saying I was being investigated by the Commerce Commission because my product wasn't Natural Glow and that I'd never invented it in the first place!

All I wanted to do was work hard, make some money and pay my debts, but every time I managed to pick myself up, someone was knocking me back down again. I knew who it was, and I wondered how low they would stoop to ruin me. I didn't have the energy or the money to keep fighting.

Money, money, money

Arnold Schwarzenegger said, 'Money doesn't make you happy. I have fifty million dollars, but I was just as happy when I had forty-eight million dollars.'

Over the years I've often been asked, 'When did you feel you were rich? When did you have enough money?' For me, it is when I can always pay the bills at the end of every month. It's when there's no uncertainty – when I feel no worry at all, no stress in the slightest, even if, for example, I have to unexpectedly take Walnut to the vet, or I have to go to the dentist.

Knowing the money is always there to pay for all the basics is to feel rich.

Money doesn't buy you happiness – that's true. But it can buy you peace of mind, freedom, security and power.

God give me patience – but give it to me now!

I think that you always get what you want, but you might not always get it when you want to – it's all about timing.

I always used to wish I'd met Duncan when we were both younger, but he says he was a different person then. I was different then, too, and it wouldn't have worked out. When we finally met each other, it was the right time for both of us. We needed each other.

So, it was the wrong timing for my TV show – the budget had already been spent.

If things had worked out three years before, I would have been in the first series of *Dancing with the Stars*. As it turned out, the third series was much better timing for me, both personally and professionally. I know I wouldn't have been able to win that first year – my motivation and determination to win wouldn't have been strong enough to get me through.

Get mad, get even madder and then get even

You can use anger in a positive way to spur you on to greater things. I've had some of my greatest successes when I've had an I'll-show-them attitude.

If people make you mad enough, there's no greater feeling than success.

The need to prove someone wrong can make you move mountains, or dance with a broken rib – we can all do anything if our motivation is strong enough.

When someone does you wrong, don't sit at home playing the same old record in your head: 'He said this. I can't believe she did that. Why can't I do the other?' Instead of being trapped by all that negative energy, I turn it into positive energy and you can, too.

Put a smile on your dial.
Make a plan.
Take one small step and then another.
Make sure you find something to laugh about every day.
Be thankful for what you have.

And, finally, trust that whoever has made you mad will get what they deserve in the end. They always do!

I've had some of my greatest successes when I've had an I'll-show-them attitude.

Notes

NEXT WEEK'S
FISH 'N' CHIP PAPER

15

But wait, there's more!

After Girls' Day Out and the terrible publicity at the time, I had a couple of really bad days when I thought, 'What's the point?' Every time there was a light at the end of the tunnel, it turned out to be an oncoming train.

But, reading again what I've written here, it reminds me of all the obstacles I've already faced and overcome in my life. And if I couldn't get over the obstacles, I went around them or through them, or I pushed them out of my way.

And I think, 'I can do that again and again if I have to.'

I will survive!

I'm not superwoman. I get hurt and angry just like everyone else. I lose hope and give up. But it's like falling off the wagon – you need to get back on again as soon as you can. It's the same when you're on a diet and you have a bad day and pig out – it doesn't matter that you've failed for one day. It's not the end of the journey and you can start your journey again tomorrow.

We all make mistakes and we all have problems. If you have no problems, you have no life.

That's all business is – solving problems. If it were just about good ideas, forecasts and budgets, everyone would be successful. It's not. It's about seeing the problem and solving it quickly.

And when the unexpected happens and it feels as if everything is going down the pan, pick this book up and read it again. You'll be able to get things moving and have another go.

Remember, life's winners aren't people any smarter or any luckier than you or me – they're just people who keep having another go.

And remember to live each day as if it's your last, because one day it will be.

Have another go

Duncan and I already have the plans in our minds for the new house we're going to build. Every now and then I might change some minor detail, like moving the outdoor spa nearer the bedroom so we can sit in it at night and look at the stars. I imagine us sitting in the bubbling hot water looking up at a beautiful night sky.

I can't wait to drive my new Mercedes convertible along the waterfront with the wind in my hair – it's going to be gold with a cream leather interior even though Walnut the Wonder Dog will have her muddy feet all over it. I don't care. That's what I'm having.

And I'm building an empire that will mean I never have to worry about money ever again. I won't owe anyone anything. I'll have enough money to do whatever I want, when I want to.

But the thing I'm really looking forward to most is going on the *Oprah Winfrey Show* with this book. The thought of it has kept me going through some dark days and I know this book will help others when they're going through theirs. That's what it's all about at the end of the day – helping people who aren't able to make it on their own. You don't have to help everyone, just someone, and the world will be a better place.

That's all
business is —
solving problems.

16

How to lay out your journal

Every New Year I start a new journal. The first thing I do is write a list at the back under the heading Personal Goals of things that I want to achieve.

Remember, you don't have to know all the ins and outs of how, where or when. Just write down anything you fancy doing or anything you want to stop doing.

Your list might look something like this:

PERSONAL GOALS
Learn sign language
Take up kung fu
Learn to play piano
Eat more healthily
Give up smoking
Apply for promotion
Read more books
Learn swing dancing
Do more scrap-booking
Learn to ride a horse
Spend more time with my family
Write a book
Take up golf
Have own TV show
Become a nurse
Go back to university.

On another page, I make another list under the heading Financial Goals. These could be long-term goals or more immediate ones regarding my day-to-day finances, or things I want to own. That list might look something like this:

FINANCIAL GOALS
Pay off all debts
Save for a holiday
Build my own home
Save for retirement
Buy a new car
Buy new lounge furniture
Have cosmetic surgery
Buy Mum a retirement apartment

Launch grocery range
Do motivational speaking
Earn x dollars
Send Dad on a holiday
Set up education funds for the kids
Launch my own website and shopping channel
Have my own range of shoes and accessories
Launch my own clothing range.

Remember, you don't have to know how you're going to achieve these goals. When you work out what you want and why, your brain will work out the how, later.

Then I study both my lists and pick the five most important things from each that I want to get moving during the year ahead. Then go to the front of my journal and write them on the first page.

The first page of your journal might look like this:

1 JANUARY 2009
Learn swing dancing
Write a motivational book
Learn to play piano
Have own TV show
Do more scrap-booking
Buy a new car
Pay off all debts
Have cosmetic surgery
Send Dad on holiday
Eat more healthily.

Whenever I have time on my hands to sit and be sad or miserable, I look at my list and do something from that instead.

I might do some scrap-booking or make a salad or do some research on the computer.

Continuing with setting up my journal, I take goal number one and list the reasons why I want to achieve that goal or how it will make me feel. For example:

1) LEARN SWING DANCING

It's something Duncan and I can do together
It takes a lot of energy so I'll lose weight
It will help tone my whole body
It will be lots of fun and there'll be lots of laughter
We can go with friends and enjoy a new hobby together
It's a great way to burn off steam
It's very social scene with lots of dances
It won't cost a lot
Duncan and I will be able to dance together at social events
It will make us feel alive and full of energy afterwards
It will surprise people when they see us doing it
It will be another string to my bow.

When it's raining outside and you can't be bothered, reading your journal and thinking about the reasons why you want to do something will spur you on.

Continuing on, I make a heading on each of the following twelve pages for the months of year: January, February, March, and so on.

I repeat this exercise for the other nine goals on my list for the year ahead.

For example:

2) WRITE A MOTIVATIONAL BOOK

It will motivate me as I'm writing it

It will set the record straight
It will help people pick themselves up
It will earn me pots of money
It will be an achievement
I will be able to use it in my motivational speaking
It will inspire people to achieve great things
I could go on *Oprah* and give away copies.

Again, at the top of the following twelve pages write the months of the year.

It may take you a few days to set up your journal, but that doesn't matter. It will change your life for ever, so what's a few days?

Once you have finished writing out all your goals and reasons why you want to achieve them, go back to the first goal and make a rough plan of what you might need to do each month. For example:

JANUARY
1) LEARN SWING DANCING
Talk my partner into it
Ask friends to go
Find a class
Book some lessons.

Then write down one step you can take right now to get things moving. For example:

Look in Yellow Pages for classes.

Now, here's the important bit – follow through right now. Go and get the Yellow Pages and look up swing dancing. You only ever have to take one small step at a time, and when you've taken it the next step will then become clear. If you don't have time to take the next step, write it in your journal ready for next time. For example:

Have a look at website.

I like to keep all my goals moving forward a bit at a time, but occasionally if I'm up against a deadline, like submitting a manuscript to a publisher, I just keep taking one small step after another on the same goal until I have achieved that goal, before looking at my other goals. For example:

2) WRITE A MOTIVATIONAL BOOK
Find a publisher
Check what books are already available
Think of a title and jot down ideas for content
Set aside time to write.

Again, I wrote down one step I could take, to move things forward:

Go to the library and look at motivational books already out there.

Once you get used to writing your goals down and the steps you can take to get things started and keep them moving you'll be amazed at what you will be able to achieve.

Keeping a journal will give you the power to turn your dreams into reality. And you don't have to wait for a new year to begin – there is no better time to start than now.

Acknowledgements

Karen Kay. Thank you, Karen, for always believing in me and for going above and beyond the call of duty.

Iain Smith and Andy at Me Salon. Thanks for the fabulous hairdos. You guys rock!

Stefano. What can I say? You turned me into a dancing queen and changed my life. You're a star!

Walnut the Wonder Dog. You are the funniest, cleverest dog in the whole wide world. You make me smile every day.

Willie, Rick and Ed. Your mother must be so proud of you all. Thank you for so many things.

Kate Dowman and team, you made it possible for me to have such a beautiful wedding dress and I thank you all.

Connie and Chap. You helped us through some tough times and I shall be forever grateful.

Kevin and Glenna. Thank you for being there when we needed you.

Sarah Nealon. I don't think I would ever have started this book without your help and encouragement, you're a lovely lady.

My brother Bill. Thanks Bill for all the great design work you did, even when you knew I couldn't pay you.

Wayne and Fleur, great Scorpios and great friends, I'm so glad we're neighbours.

Mike Denny. You're always there when we need you. Always the gentleman.

For my friends Vicky and Kathy, you've always been there for me and made me laugh when I didn't feel like it.

Deborah Kelleher. Dancing with the Stars came along just when I needed it – thank you so much for making that dream come true.

Thanks Mum for never complaining when things go wrong and for always being on my side.

Dear old Dad, I miss you every day and wish you lived here with me. Thank God for the lovely Edna to look after you.

Our Phil, we had some bad times and I'm so proud of you, for making it on your own and creating a wonderful family life with Pat and the boys.

And a huge thank you to the New Zealand public for making me feel at home and lifting my spirits every day.